THE NEW COCKER SPANIEL

Ch. Scioto Bluff's Sin-Bahr, Ch. Scioto Bluff's Sinbad and Ch. Pounette Scioto Bluff's Sibyl. Sinbad, whelped in 1959, stands as the leading sire of the breed with 118 champions. He was bred and owned by Charles D. and Veda L. Winders.

The NEW
Cocker
Spaniel

by RUTH M. KRAEUCHI

FIRST EDITION
Sixth Printing — 1983

HOWELL BOOK HOUSE Inc.
230 Park Avenue
New York, N.Y. 10169

Library of Congress Cataloging in Publication Data

Kraeuchi, Ruth.
  The New Cocker Spaniel.

  Bibliography: p. 288
  1. Cocker spaniels. I. Title.
SF429.C55K73   636.7'52   78-12698
ISBN 0-87605-104-2

*This book is dedicated to
the memory of the many wonderful
Cocker Spaniels I have known
during the past forty years.*

Ruth Kraeuchi (pronounced Cracky) was born in St. Joseph, Missouri, and it was there that she had her first contact with a Cocker Spaniel. An aunt came for a visit and brought along her pet, a Cocker, and the impression made has remained with Ruth all her lifetime.

Years later, after they had moved from an apartment in St. Louis to the spacious grounds of a small farm near the city, her husband Lee presented her with a little black Cocker puppy as a Christmas gift. She was not a show dog but did have long black ears and lots of shiny black coat and Ruth was smitten. At that time the couple had no idea of becoming deeply involved with dogs, though they were very fond of Lee's hunting dogs. Lee had an electric retail business in downtown St. Louis, and Ruth had become a convention reporter, a work that developed her interest in writing.

As their interest in Cocker Spaniels increased, Lee decided to turn the large barn into a kennel. This "small" kennel grew by leaps and bounds. Lee then decided to add handling to his other activities and he was soon a professional. The retail business was sold and Lee devoted all of his time to the kennel and handling. Ruth became his assistant.

The kennel work became more and more demanding, and while Lee had excellent success as a handler it soon became necessary for him to concentrate on the kennel and Ruth took over as the professional handler. Her success is evidenced by the long string of Bests in Show and Bests of Breed that her charges won.

But no matter how great one's success may be, there are always some wins one never forgets. Lee and Ruth's first home-bred champion, Silver Maple Sensation, gave them a thrill that will never be relived. Ruth's win of Best in Show at the National Specialty in 1969 (with Ch. Dream Echo Magic Touch), her Quaker Oats Award with Ch. Silver Maple Doctor David, and her triumphs with the co-owned Ch. Burson's Blarney (top winning Cocker in the Nation for two years in a row) all remain fresh thrills.

Lee Kraeuchi was Zone Representative for Zone 3 the first four years after it was established in 1946. In 1963 Ruth was elected to the office and served diligently through 1973—12 years of devotion to the American Spaniel Club and the breed.

In the early 1950s, Ruth wrote a book on Cocker Spaniels that was published by the Judy Publishing Company. She wrote the breed column in the *AKC Gazette* for six years, and then started a column which appeared in *Dog World* for 14 years. The column was titled "What the Judge Wants in the Cocker Ring" and was very popular not only with Cocker fanciers, but with all Sporting dog enthusiasts. It provided a rich background for this book in that in writing it, Ruth regularly contacted every judge licensed to judge Cockers.

A very bad automobile accident in the sixties curtailed Lee's activities, and he is today confined to a wheel chair. But he continues his interest in the Cockers and in Ruth's activities with the dog sport.

Contents

Foreword   11
    by Herbert D. Roling

Where It's At for the Cocker Spaniel   14

Acknowledgments   15

Introduction   17

1. Origin and Early History   21

> The Spaniel Family, 21
> Division into Varieties, 22
> The First Shows, 22

2. The Cocker Spaniel Comes to America   27

> First Champions of the Breed, 27
> Early American Breeders, 29
> The 1920s to the 1950s, 31
> Famous Cocker Handlers, 35
> Resurgence—The Up and Down (and Up Again)
> of Cocker Registrations, 37

3. Breed Type   39
    Text and drawings by Ron Fabis

> "Cocker of the Year"—1960 to 1977-   45
> a pictorial presentation.

4. The Modern Cocker Spaniel in America   57

> Featuring kennels that have produced
> outstanding Cocker Spaniels in the years
> since 1950:
> Winders, 57; Orient, 58; Dreamridge, 58;
> Nor-Mar, 61; Davis, 62; Artru, 64; Rex-
> pointe, 66; Maribeau, 66; LaMar, 66;

Nosowea, 70; Petts, 70; Bleuaire, 72;
Thompson, 72; Golden Acre, 72; Dur-
Bet, 76; Biggs, 76; Priority, 79; Clark-
dale, 80; Har-Dee, 80; Shardeloes, 80;
My-Ida-Ho, 82; Kobbytown, 82; Camp-
bell, 82; Sandrex, 84; Kaplar's, 84; Wib's,
84; Seven Acres, 88; Charberson, 88;
Earnscliffe, 88; Plantation, 88; Gina, 88;
Cameo's Dawn, 92; Deep River, 92;
Twyneff, 92; Loch Lane, 92; Butch, 92;
Ca-Da, 94; Juniper, 94; Forjay, 94; Can-
dylane, 94; Breezy Hill, 96; Robin Knoll,
96; Rinky Dink, 96; Hob-Nob, 98; Hey-
day, 98; Jersie Hill, 100; Seenar, 100;
Van-Dor, 100; Main-Dale, 100; Dream
Echo, 100; Magicour, 104; Birchwood,
104; Glen Hollow, 104; Fi-Fo, 104;
Silver Maple, 104; Marley, 104; Maas,
106; Hall-Way, 106; Flintcrest, 106; Jo-
Be-Glen, 106; Camby, 108; Harlanha-
ven, 108; Reno, 108; Liz-Bar, 108;
Kekko, 108; Merryhaven, 110; Forbes,
110; Lurola, 110; Valli-Lo, 110; Hi-
Boots, 114; BeGay, 114; Baliwick, 114;
Champagne, 114; Shiloh Dell, 114; Phi-
Tau, 116; Bobwin, 116; Mijo's, 116;
Corwin, 116; Milru, 116; Alorah, 116;
Sagamore, 116; Windy Hill, 120; Lane-
brook, 120; Laurim, 120; Velasco, 120;
Sanstar, 120; Tabaka, 120; Russ, 124;
Frandee, 124.

The Top Producers   127
     A pictorial presentation, with pedigrees.

5. Cocker Spaniel Colors   147
     The Story of the "Browns," 149
     by Arlene Swalwell

6. The Cocker Spaniel in Canada   157
     by Mrs. Norma Donderwitz
     The Cocker Spaniel in Western Canada, 161
     by Maxine Norris

7. The American Cocker in Other Countries   165
     Great Britain, *by Muriel and Andrew Caine,* 165
     Holland, *by Marilyn W. Pryor,* 168
     France, *by Marilyn W. Pryor,* 171
     Mexico, *by Owen L. Young,* 176
     South America, *by Owen L. Young,* 178
     Japan, *by Miko Takanashi,* 178

8. Official AKC Standard for the Cocker Spaniel   185

    Pictorial Visualization, Black—184
    Pictorial Visualization, ASCOB—186
    Pictorial Visualization, Parti—188
    Anatomy of the Cocker Spaniel, 192
    by Robert F. Way, V.M.D., M.S.

9. The Standard Examined in Depth   197

    Skull, 198; Eyes, 200; Ears, 200; Neck
    and Shoulders, 200; Body, 203; Tail, 203;
    Legs and Feet, 205; Coat, 205; Color and
    Markings, 205; Movement, 206.

10. Choosing a Cocker Spaniel Puppy   211

    What to look for in buying a puppy,
    whether for pet or show:
       At 3 weeks, 212
       At 2 months, 212
       At 4 months, 214
       At 6 months, 216
       At 9 months, 216

11. Grooming the Cocker for Show   221
    Drawings by Peggy Bang

12. How to Show the Cocker Spaniel   235

13. Care and Training of the Cocker Spaniel   247

    Coat Care, 247
    Grooming the Pet, 250
    Summer Care, 252
    Feeding Your Cocker, 254
    Care of the Stud Dog and Brood Bitch, 254
    Training Your Pet, 255
    The Comfort of Your Cocker, 257

14. The Cocker Spaniel in Obedience   259
    by John S. Ward

    Temperament, 260
    Training for Obedience Trials, 263
    Conformation vs. Obedience, 265
    Tracking, 268
    Some Notable Obedience Cockers, 269

15. The Cocker Spaniel as a Hunting Dog   271

    Today's Cocker in the Field, 273
    by Frank S. Wood

16. Cocker Spaniel Clubs   281

    Bibliography   288

Mr. Herbert D. Roling is pictured (left) awarding First in Sporting Group at Staten Island KC's 1978 show to Am. and Can. Ch. Tabaka's Tidbit O'Wynden, CD. Handled by Ted Young, Jr. (center). Awarding the trophy is Dr. Wolfgang Casper. Tidbit went on to Best in Show. The winner of the 1978 American Spaniel Club February Specialty, she was winning Groups and Bests in Show at a pace that put her—at this writing—well in front for "Cocker of the Year" honors. Owned by Laura Watt O'Connor and Ruth Tabaka.

10

Foreword

The author and publisher are honored to have this Foreword by Mr. Herbert D. Roling, past president of the American Spaniel Club (1964-1967) and its current delegate to the American Kennel Club. Mr. Roling has been a member of the Board of the ASC since 1945, serving continually on many committees and/or as elected officer, including 11 years as Treasurer and the two terms as President.

Along with his service with the parent club, Mr. Roling has been president of the Cocker Spaniel Club of Long Island, the Connecticut-Westchester Cocker Spaniel Club and the Meadowbrook Cocker Spaniel Club. He recently retired as president of the Elm City Kennel Club (all-breeds).

He registered his first Cocker Spaniel litter around 1930. He became an AKC judge approved to do all Spaniels in the mid-40s and for many years now has been approved to judge all dogs of the Sporting Group.

Mr. Roling compiled the treasured 1959 hardbound annual of the American Spaniel Club. Earlier, he had assisted in compiling the 1946 hardbound annual.

Wɪᴛʜ the American Cocker Spaniel's recapture of first place in the hearts of Sporting dog fanciers, there is obvious need and appropriateness for an up-to-date, complete, honest and authoritative text on the breed.

Today's Cocker Spaniel is better in quality, conformation to the standard and temperament than any in the past. The tendency toward more and more coat has been checked by a more explicit wording in the Standard, and there has been a rekindling of interest in the American Cocker as a hunting or field dog. Overbreeding has been arrested. *The New Cocker Spaniel*, written by Ruth Kraeuchi and published by Howell Book House Inc., provides the much needed updating.

I have known Ruth and her husband Lee for over 40 years and through those years have shared with them an intense admiration for the breed and a dedication to its well being and progress. Ruth is a legend in her own time and is the epitome of the successful breeder, exhibitor, handler and writer. I can think of no one whose experience has been more rounded or extensive. She has been one of the most respected handlers since the 1930s and has piloted outstanding dogs of all varieties to success.

Lee and Ruth were pioneers in the establishment of Zone 3 in the American Spaniel Club framework. Lee has hunted over Cockers virtually all of his life. Their Silver Maple Kennels is one of the most honored prefixes and dogs that they have bred have been the foundations of some of our foremost kennels. At the 7th annual Zone 3 show in St. Louis in 1953, Ch. Silver Maple Doctor David, ASCOB, was Best in Show after winning his 100th Best of Variety, and then was retired with an unprecedented record for Cockers of any variety.

Ruth has been a steadying influence on the ASC's Standard Committee and in recent years her expertise in the breed has made her one of our most highly respected, most sought after judges. She still finds the American Cocker the most exciting dog to watch in the show ring and has guided many novices in their first steps in the sport. Countless helpful articles on all phases of Cockerdom, as well as an earlier book on the breed, have been written by her.

Yet, characteristic of her modesty, she has not hesitated to turn to others for help with phases in which her experience has not been as extensive. In selecting John S. (Jack) Ward to write the Obedience chapter and Frank Wood and Evelyn Monte Van Horn to help with the Field Dog chapter, she has considerably enriched the book's serviceability.

The New Cocker Spaniel emphasizes the important producers and their pedigrees. The over 250 pictures that trace the American Cocker right up to now provide many happy memories for us old-timers; for the newcomer they afford generations of bloodlines as guidelines, not heretofore available in one book.

12

Through the years Ruth and I have seen most things eye-to-eye. We are in full agreement that the main ingredient in the Cocker's current status is the emphasis placed by the breeders on temperament in recent years. The Cocker's merry disposition, above all, is the essence of the breed. I join with her in the hope that the resurgence in popularity will not result in any downgrading of top quality and sunny dispositions.

One can only hope that the breed will continue to move in this direction. Enlightened breeders and judges can do much to sustain this. Because it is sure to make more knowledgeable breeders and judges of its readers, I salute *The New Cocker Spaniel* and wish it great success.

—HERBERT D. ROLING

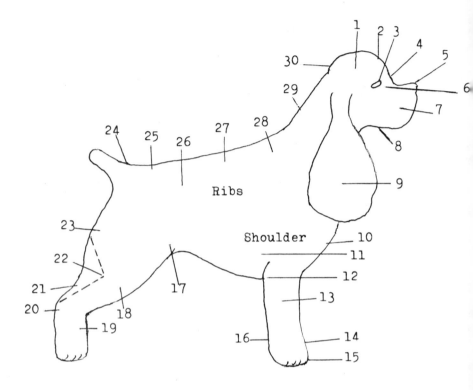

Where It's At for the Cocker Spaniel

1. Skull	11. Brisket	21. Lower Thigh
2. Forehead	12. Elbow	22. Angulation
3. Eye	13. Foreleg	23. Upper Thigh
4. Stop	14. Paw	24. Tail Set
5. Nose	15. Pad	25. Croup
6. Chiseling	16. Pastern	26. Loin
7. Muzzle	17. Tuck-up	27. Back
8. Jaw	18. Stifle	28. Withers
9. Ear	19. Hock	29. Neck
10. Forechest	20. Hock Joint	30. Occiput

Acknowledgments

M Y VERY SPECIAL THANKS to those who have so graciously contributed materials that richly add to this book:

Herbert D. Roling is one of the most respected figures in the dog sport and I am honored to have his Foreword.

John S. Ward is a member of the Board of Directors of the American Kennel Club. His chapter on the Cocker in Obedience is a masterful one—informative and authoritative. We treasure it.

Arlene Swalwell has given the fancy interesting information on the development of the popular chocolate Cocker Spaniels. Evelyn Monte Van Horn and Frank S. Wood have contributed excellent information on the Cocker in the field. For their fine contributions on "Cockers in Other Countries" we are indebted to: Muriel and Andrew Caine (England); Marilyn W. Prior (Holland and France); Owen L. Young (Mexico and South America); Norma Donderwitz and Maxine Norris (Canada) and Mikio Takanashi (Japan).

We appreciate the cooperation of the copyright holders in allowing us to reprint: Breed Type (text and drawings by Ron Fabis) from *The American Cocker Spaniel*, © 1976 by the American Spaniel Club; the Visualizations of the Standard and Anatomy of the Cocker Spaniel (drawings by Robert F. Way, V.M.D., B.S.) from *Dog Standards Illustrated*, © 1975 by Howell Book House Inc.

My appreciation, too, to Ron Fabis, Judith Graham and Ted Young for their help in reviewing and assembling the contents of this book.

—RUTH M. KRAEUCHI

Cocker appeal, personified by Ch. Rob-Mar's Jack Frost.

Introduction

Today's cocker spaniel bears little resemblance to his ancestors. The improvement in appearance, size and temperament over the last fifty years has been astounding.

Today's Cocker is right in size. His beauty is breathtaking. But most important of all, he is a dog of superb disposition. The Cocker's ideal temperament today is its own testament to the success of the dedicated breeders who made this their paramount goal through the years.

The character of the Cocker Spaniel is founded on his love of people. When they return his affection, he appears to prefer the human race over even members of his own canine family.

The Cocker's greatest popularity is as a house pet. He is an ideal family dog—adaptable to all situations. Whether in a very small apartment or a large house with spacious grounds, he will adjust his daily life to that of his owner. He can be a happy walking companion, or will quickly learn to ride in an automobile.

The Cocker is wonderful with children and enjoys playing with them. However, here a word of caution is in order. Parents should teach their children how to properly handle the dog. Excessive roughness or teasing is not good and will often ruin an otherwise excellent disposition. When the playtime is too rough, the Cocker will learn to respond in a similar manner.

Today's Cocker is a happy dog at heart and should be given every chance to prove it. His record as an obedience dog is excellent and his love for the work is shown by his merry tail.

Love of the Cocker starts early.

He remains very popular as a hunting dog. Although he is not used as extensively as some of the larger breeds, he has the ability to retrieve and the nose to find the game. He loves to be out of doors, not only to hunt but to be with his master and his family.

As a show dog, the Cocker is unsurpassed. He is easily trained and is very cooperative. There is nothing more beautiful than a properly groomed Cocker, trained to move out with style, holding his own with the larger dogs of the Sporting Group. Usually, if there is applause, he seems inspired to throw his head higher and prance. He makes a truly spectacular picture and seems fully aware of it.

Small wonder then that he is today again the No. 1 in popularity of all Sporting dogs.

Playtime.

Woodcock shooting.

1

Origin and
Early History

THE NAME SPANIEL was known as long ago as 1328. General opinion is that this dog family originated in Spain. There is no definite evidence to indicate that they could not have been brought into Spain from the East. However, most writings speak strongly of Spain as the place of origin—hence the name "Spaniel."

The first mention of the Spaniel in English literature was in 1340. "For as a Spanyel she wol on him lepe" is found in Chaucer's *Wif of Bathe's Prologue*. This indicates that the breed was familiar to the English over six centuries ago. In 1368, there was again mention of the "Spanyell" in English books.

The writings of the French Count, Gaston de Foix, in 1387, indicate that the Spaniel was well known in his locality which was near the border of Spain.

In *The Master of Game,* a work written between 1406 and 1413, by Edward, the Second Duke of York, we have another suggestion that the breed was Spanish. "Hounds for the hawk, Spaniels, that came from Spain" was written by this authority, to which he added, "notwithstanding, there were many in other countries." This would indicate that he was a little doubtful of their origin.

There is much written of the Spaniels hunting ability and of their merry dispositions. While we see great difference in the appearance of the early Spaniels and today's Cocker Spaniels, these characteristics have carried through the years. In early writings, there is mention of their wagging tails when running before their master, raising and starting fowl.

They also acted as "Couchers" (Setters), helping in this manner to take both partridges and quail with a net. The way sportsmen hunted in those days was to go over the fields with a net, their hawks above keeping the game close to the ground. The game dared not move lest the hawks see them. The Spaniels, on scenting game, turned in the direction in which the game was hiding. The hawks kept the game from rising and the dogs got very near to the birds. The Spaniels were trained to "go down" while the hunters placed the net over the birds.

Spaniels of that day were used extensively in recovering wounded water fowl as they were excellent swimmers.

Bewick, in 1790, describes the large Water Spaniel as a "beautiful animal" remarkable for docility, obedience and attachment to the master. Also, "elegant" in shape, with "beautifully curled or crisped" hair.

Bewick also describes a smaller variety, similar to the large Water Spaniel, but shorter on leg. He describes this dog as one with feet of exaggerated length.

Later the gun took the place of the falcon and the net for the sportsmen. Because of the time needed for loading and aiming, the very lively Water Spaniel did not work satisfactorily. The hunters found need for a smaller Spaniel with shorter legs. This was the beginning of a separation in the Spaniel family. The Spaniels were then divided into just two varieties: the land and the water Spaniels. Later, there was further separation and the terms Springer, Springing Spaniel, Cocker, Cocking Spaniel and Cock Flusher came into use. The name Cocker was applied to the smallest, most compact of this group.

The First Shows

In 1859, a dog show exclusively for sporting Spaniels was held in Birmingham, England, and there was a class for Cockers. But following this, the name "Cocker" was discontinued as a class in the shows. About seven years later the Spaniel classes were divided into Large Size and Small Size and Cockers were eligible for the Small Size.

No further effort was made to divide the classes to include the Cocker and by 1874, the Cocker was shown as a Field Spaniel. In 1875, the Crystal Palace Show Committee gave classes for "Sussex, Clumber, Other large breeds of Spaniels and Other small breeds of Spaniels."

Field Trial Ch. Rivington Sam, famous British Cocker owned by C. A. Phillips of Scotland, one of the leading breeders of the late 1800s.–From a painting by R. Ward Binks.

Braeside Bustle, a leading winner of the 1890s in England, owned by H.S. Lloyd of Ware. Described as "a black and white and black and blue flecked dog".

Ch. Rivington Robena.

Ch. Obo and Miss Obo, bred and owned by James Farrow of England. Obo, whelped June 14, 1879, gave name to one of the important founding strains of American Cockers. He is recorded to have weighed 22 pounds and to have been 10″ in height. Length from nose to set-on of tail was 29″.

Ch. Lily Obo. Owner James Farrow of England stated in the 1890s that "Lily was considered by most of our expert Spaniel judges as the most typical of perfect Cockers ever exhibited."

Cocker Spaniel history really began about 1883. At the Ashton show that year, a class for Cocker Spaniels was given, and James Farrow showed Obo, Miss Obo and Sally Obo. A class was also held for Cockers at Hertford that year, and the following year, Margate held such a class.

Some of the larger clubs were slow to recognize the breed. Crystal Palace and Birmingham ignored them until a letter in the press questioned why such an important breed as the Cocker Spaniel did not have a class.

It was then that the Kennel Club acted. The fact that Cockers had been winning, made it necessary to give them a place in the Kennel Club Stud Book. Their classification read: "Field, other than liver-colored, exceeding 25 lbs., and Cockers, any color, not exceeding 25 lbs."

This was the beginning of the inclusion of Cocker classes in the English shows. There followed much confusion in names as Field Spaniels were often included in the same class as Cockers with the weight stipulation the only distinguishing factor.

It was not until 1892 that the Kennel Club of England gave a classification for Cockers only. Many of the active breeders of that time bred dogs and bitches whose bloodlines will be found in some of the extended pedigrees of Cocker Spaniels that came later in America. These include the Obo line, the Rivington bloodline, the Bruton line, the Bowdler line and others.

Ch. Ted Obo, an 1897 English champion, bred and owned by James Farrow of Ipswich, England. A son of Ch. Lily Obo.

Ch. Obo II, whelped in 1882, is often called the "father" of the American Cocker. By Obo ex Chloe II (who was imported in whelp), he was purchased as a puppy and raised in New Hampshire by J. P. Willey. Obo II was the first of the Obo strain to reach this country.

Red Brucie, whelped in 1921, was the outstanding sire of his time. Bred and owned by Herman Mellenthin, he sired 38 champions that included many foundation dogs. At one point of the 1930s it was calculated that 90% of the successful show Cockers and 85% of the field Cockers were traceable to him.

2

The Cocker Spaniel Comes to America

IN 1879, the National American Kennel Club, later to become the American Kennel Club, published its first Stud Book in St. Louis, Missouri.

The first Cocker registered in America was a liver and white named Captain and was registered under the number 1354.

The first black and tan registered in America was Jockey. His number was 1365.

In Volume II of the Stud Book, published in 1885, Brush II was registered under the number 3124. This Cocker was imported by the Comming's Cocker Spaniel Kennel of Asworth, N. H. He was described as the ideal of that period. However, his popularity was not great with the American fancy.

The first orange and white Cocker registered was Fritz, number 4301, appearing in Volume III.

The first red registered was Little Red Rover, a daughter of Obo II, and registered as number 5869.

The first black and white parti-color registered was a bitch named Daffodil, number 4312, whelped May 13, 1881. Her registration certificate appeared as "Black, white-ticked."

The historic early dog of the breed in America was Ch. Obo II, No. 4911, whelped in 1882, a son of the original Obo owned by James Far-

Ch. Midkiff Miracle Man, Specialty winner of the mid-20's. By Robinhurst Foreglow out of Midkiff Seductive (Westminster BIS 1921). Owned by the L'Hommedieus' Sand Spring Kennels.

Ch. Lucknow Creme de la Creme, whelped 1925, a Specialty and Group winner owned by Mr. and Mrs. Fred Brown.

Ch. Sand Spring Surmise, a red son of Foreglow, whelped 1924. Surmise was the foundation dog for Sand Spring Kennels.

row of England. The breeder is identified as F. F. Pitcher. Obo II's dam (Chloe II) had been imported in whelp and he was purchased as a puppy and named by J. P. Willey of New Hampshire.

This black dog was probably the first stud dog to establish a definite strain. While his conformation was quite different from Cockers of today, there is no doubt as to his worth as a foundation for the breed in America.

His half sister, Miss Obo II, was highly praised and her producing ability also contributed toward the elevation of the Cocker. The fact that both Obo II and Miss Obo II were ancestors of the great Robinhurst Foreglow establishes their producing fame.

Robinhurst Foreglow, owned by Judge Townsend Scudder, was a son of Blackstone Chief. In order to buy Chief, it was necessary for Judge Scudder to buy the entire Blackstone Kennel of 32 dogs. The purchase proved worthwhile, for Chief was the sire of Foreglow, who in turn was sire of Red Brucie, Ch. Sand Spring Surmise, Ch. Midkiff Miracle Man and Canadian Ch. Limestone Laddie. Through these four dogs, Robinhurst Foreglow's blood is carried to most Cockers of today, as extended pedigrees will show.

In Robinhurst Foreglow, Judge Scudder saw a sire that would be of great value in improving the breed. For this reason, he offered a free stud service to anyone owning a typical Cocker bitch. Some hesitated to take advantage of this offer as Foreglow was different from the long, low Cockers they were used to seeing.

However, two breeders, William T. Payne of the Midkiff Kennels of Pennsylvania, and Herman Mellenthin of Poughkeepsie, N. Y., were more far-seeing than the others and realized that there was going to be a change in the appearance of the Cocker. Both took advantage of Judge Scudder's offer and history was made.

Mr. Payne acquired Robinhurst Foreglow later on and he became a great influence in the Midkiff Kennels. Red Brucie, bred by Herman Mellenthin in 1921, generally recognized as his greatest son, sired 38 champions, a great number for that period. Another great son of Foreglow was Ch. Sand Spring Surmise, whelped in 1924. He became the foundation of the Sand Spring Kennel.

From the early 1900s on, Cocker Spaniel popularity experienced a steady, uninterrupted growth that was to bloom through five decades. Pioneers of the period included: Mr. Bloodgood, Mepal Kennels; George Greer, Brookside Kennels; E. W. Fiske, Mount Vernon Kennels; Mrs. Warner, Belle Isle Kennels and Mrs. Haley Fiske, Overcross Kennels. The earliest pioneer on the West Coast was Governor James Rolph who established his Mission Kennels in 1908.

Ch. Idahurst Belle II, Best in Show at the 1930, 1931 and 1932 ASC Specialties. Bred and owned by O. B. Gilman.

Ch. Holmeric of Brookville, whelped 1937, sire of 19 champions. Owned by Mr. and Mrs. E. D. Stringfellow.

Ch. My Own Today, 1930 Specialty winner, owned by Miss Alice Dodsworth's Windsweep Kennels. My Own Today had been purchased as a virtually unshown bitch from Herman Mellenthin for $5000.

Judge Scudder's contributions to the breed were monumental. He had acquired his first Cocker Spaniel in 1880 and was a founding member of the American Spaniel Club in 1881. A great judge of the bench widely known for his many courageous decisions, he still found time for seventy years of dedication to the Cocker Spaniel. Indicative of the span of his services, he was president of the ASC in 1920, and again in 1944. He was the guiding light over a long era, and when he finally decided to step down because of his age, he was immediately elected President Emeritus, which honor he held until he passed on.

In 1921, Mr. Payne's black and white parti-color Ch. Midkiff Seductive, became the first Cocker to win Best in Show at Westminster in Madison Square Garden, New York City. (Other Cockers to have since won this honor are Ch. My Own Brucie in 1940 and 1941 and Ch. Carmor's Rise and Shine in 1954.)

The Cocker Spaniel picture developed rapidly during the '20s and '30s. Along with Mr. Payne and Mr. Mellenthin, very active breeders included: O. B. Gilman, Idahurst Kennels; Miss Dodsworth, Windsweep Kennels; Mr. and Mrs. Macy Willetts, Cassilis and Mepals; Mrs. W. Morgan Churchman and Mr. E. W. Clark; Mr. and Mrs. S. Y. L'Hommedieu of Sand Spring Kennels; Mrs. Elizabeth Brown, Tokalon Kennels; the Duryeas of Wilmarland Kennels; Lattimer Rees; Mrs. Arthur Vogel (later Mrs. Mathew Imrie), Freeland Kennels; C. A. Backus, Huntington Kennels; Mrs. George Anderson, Mardormere Kennels; Mrs. Frances F. Garvan, Dungarvan Kennels; Mrs. J. M. Lazear, Marjolear Kennels; Constance Wall, Argyll Kennels; Clinton Wilmerding and many more.

On the West Coast, the Knebworth Kennel of Mrs. Shute, Governor Rolph's already noted Mission Kennels, and Miss Louise Hering's Golden State Kennels produced many, many champions and their lines carried on through the years. C. B. Van Meter started his Stockdale Kennel around 1930 and it became a very active kennel. His greatest Cocker was Ch. Stockdale Town Talk, Group winner at Westminster in 1944 and sire of 87 champions, a record that stood until recent years.

The Sand Spring line became the foundation of many kennels throughout the country. Ch. Sand Spring Follow Through, whelped in 1929, sired 16 champions, one of which was our own Ch. Sand Spring Star of Stockdale, his greatest producing son. Star sired 13 champions, and was the foundation of our Silver Maple Kennels.

Another great Sand Spring dog was Stormalong (whelped in 1932), purchased by C. B. Van Meter. His show career was sensational and

Ch. Torohill Trader, whelped 1932, one of the all-time great showmen of the breed. Winner of the 1936 and 1937 ASC National Specialties. Trader as a sire is credited as having put the Cocker "up on leg." He was owned by Leonard J. Buck.

Ch. Nonquitt Notable, whelped 1935, a Best in Show winning Trader son. Bred and owned by Mrs. Henry A. Moss.

Ch. My Own Brucie, top winning Cocker of the years immediately before World War II. Bred and owned by Herman Mellenthin.

while he only lived six years, he sired 14 champions. His best producing son was Ch. Stockdale Startler; he sired 12 champions and his producing daughters were sensational. Many West Coast kennels got their start from this line.

Another outstanding kennel of the 1930s was Idahurst. The champions finished by the Gilmans' kennel are too numerous to list. Their greatest was Ch. Idahurst Belle II who won Best in Show at the National Specialty in 1930, 1931, and 1932.

Herman E. Mellenthin and his My Own Kennels became more and more important during the '30s. He had the ability through extensive breeding to come up with some of the greats, not only for himself, but for others. While the Torohill Kennels were the breeders of Ch. Torohill Trader, it was Mr. Mellenthin who arranged the mating and who owned and later sold Trader to Mr. Leonard Buck's Blackstone Kennels.

A great deal of Mr. Mellenthin's success came from breeding back into the Red Brucie strain. He was interested in all colors. He was the breeder of the great Dual Ch. My Own High Time, a parti-color foundation.

But of all the greats bred by Mr. Mellenthin, the most celebrated has been Ch. My Own Brucie. His greatest wins were Best in Show at Westminster in 1940 and 1941. Undoubtedly, this dog did more to create popular interest in the breed than any other dog.

When Herman Mellenthin passed on in 1942, the book was closed on the intermediate development of the breed. The changes that followed pertained mostly to head formation which was quite noticeable. Skulls became narrower and the entire head presented a balance between skull and foreface not seen before.

Another kennel whose work left a mark was the Scioto Kennel of Dr. James. M. Phillips. The findings of his experiments in color breeding live on. When Dr. Phillips passed away, his records were left to Louis Schmidt of the Mistwood Kennel, and became the basis for the many articles Mr. Schmidt wrote.

Another prominent breeder who was active during that era was R. Kenneth Cobb, who handled the Cockers owned by the Homeric Kennel prior to starting his own kennel which was aptly named Try Cob. Many champions were finished under the prefix Homeric as well as Try Cob.

Other prominent kennels of that time were: the Nonquitt Kennels of Mrs. Ross; the Pinefair Kennels of Mrs. H. Terrell Van Ingen; the Sugartown Kennels of Dr. and Mrs. Lewis H. Marks and the Sohio Kennels of Mr. and Mrs. Clyde Seymour.

Ch. Stockdale Town Talk, fore-
most Cocker of the era following
World War II. Owned by C. B. Van
Meter.

Ch. Sand Spring Stormalong, who
dominated the Midwest when
Trader was supreme in the East.
Sire of 14 champions, he was
owned by C. B. Van Meter.

Ch. Stockdale Startler, whelped
1935, whose 12 champion
progeny included some particularly distinguished bitches. Bred
and owned by C. B. Van Meter.

Herbert Bobb's kennel was distinguished by two great parti-colors: Ch. Bobb's Master Showman and Ch. Bobb's Show Master. Master Showman sired 32 champions and his son, Show Master sired 23 champions. These two dogs set a new pattern in parti-colors, and about 75% of the partis today carry their bloodlines.

The Honey Creek Kennels of Mrs. Beatrice W. Wegusen followed in the footsteps of Bobb's Kennels using some of its bloodlines with great success. Probably their greatest was Ch. Honey Creek Vivacious, who set a remarkable record of producing 14 champions while taking Groups and Best in Show wins.

Some other kennels that were very active during the forties and fifties, but are no longer active, were: the Bar-Nan Kennels of Mr. and Mrs. Art Friend; the Orchardlawn Kennels of Horace Harter; the Myroy Kennels of Roy Cowan; the Strathmore Kennels of William Wunderlich; the Rocky Point Kennels of Paul Berlowitz; the Blairwood Kennels of Mrs. Shiras Blair and many others in the Middle West.

Some in the South were: Elderwood; Wynnehaven; Lyonell; Young's; Hi-Tone; Hi-Pines; Murjoy; and Hilador.

On the West Coast there were: Joaquin; Swan-ee; Alfmar; Kay Emm's; Charson; Las Trampas; Bermar and others.

Those who started their activities during the forties and fifties and are still breeding actively will be covered in the next chapter.

Professional handlers have had an important role in the development of the Cocker Spaniel.

Ted Young, Jr. has handled many top Cockers including a Westminster Best in Show winner (Ch. Carmor's Rise and Shine in 1954). Probably his most celebrated has been Ch. Sagamore Toccoa, the top winning dog of all breeds in the country in 1972. Ted's dedication to the Cocker goes back to his boyhood days; his dad, Ted Sr., was one of the foremost trainers of field trial Cockers. Teddy is currently president of the Professional Handlers Association and his win of Best in Show at the 1978 National Specialty affirms that he's still with the tops in his profession. Important in Ted's success, and a fine handler on his own, has been his longtime assistant at Tedwin Kennels, Johnny Paluga.

Norman Austin's ability to present the Cocker Spaniel at its best cannot be denied. He presented Cockers to fabulous records for many years including the No. 1 dog of all breeds for 1961, Ch. Pinetop's Fancy Parade. He has also been a very successful breeder.

Clint Callahan continues active as a handler with some forty years of great success behind him. I believe Clint has been an active

Ch. Nonquitt Nola's Candidate, Best in Show at the American Spaniel Club Specialty in 1943 an[...]
1945. Bred and owned by Mrs. Henry A. Ross and handled by Kenneth Cobb. Presenting the Be[...]
in Show trophy is Mrs. Ruth Judy.

Ch. Bobb's Master Showman, left, and his son Ch. Bobb's Show Master. Showm[...]
red/white—whelped 1940, was everything his name implied in the show ring and he became sir[...]
32 champions. Show Master was sire of 23 champions. They were often shown as a brace. Bred [...]
owned by Herbert W. Bobb.

handler longer than anyone else in the breed. His wife, Dorothy, has also been a fine handler, and their mutual contribution to the progress of the breed has been tremendous.

Jim Hall is another long time handler who has had great success in the show ring. He is still active as a handler.

Art and Ruth Benhoff have not only been great handlers over many years but have contributed a great deal through their Artru Kennels breeding. Their record is fabulous and they are still very active in the show ring.

Dorothy Christiansen has been a dedicated and very successful breeder and handler for many years.

Prominent among the old-timers were Jack Gleeson, Bain and Ken Cobb, George Young, Lee and Ruth Kraeuchi. Some who are no longer with us but who will be well-remembered are: Bill Ernst, Parley Larabee and David Lowe.

Handlers identified with dedication to the breed over more recent years include Ron Fabis, Don Johnston, Terry and Charlotte Stacy, Tom Campbell, Rune Nilsson, Dee Dee Wood, Tad Duncan, Bob Covey, Ed McCauley, Micky Veno, Beth Hoffmann and Everett Dean (now retired from handling to judge).

All have had a part in building the Cocker to its present high level and deserve much credit for their efforts.

Resurgence—The Up and Down (and Up Again) of Cocker Registrations

The number of Cocker Spaniels registered by the American Kennel Club in the year 1930 was 2,528. This included the English Cocker variety for they did not become recognized as a separate breed by the AKC until September 1946.

By 1936 the annual registration total had climbed to 12,714 and the Cocker became No. 1 of all breeds in popularity. It was to hold this top position for 17 years until the Beagle took over in 1953. Top year in this span was 1947 when the Cocker registered 78,500—30% of the all-breed total, and more than three times the second ranking breed.

Such popularity can, unfortunately, have its disadvantages as well as questionable advantages. There is a tendency to get on the bandwagon when a breed becomes so popular and those interested only in sales can cause trouble. There is sure to be some indiscriminate breeding and—as a consequence—poor quality in the breed.

The Cocker's downward spiral began in 1948. In 1952 (its last year in first place) it was at 46,823. By 1955 it was third with 32,941 and by 1960 it had dropped to seventh with 17,044.

Happily, however, dedicated breeders went to work on improvement in the breed and in 1964, the Cocker's popularity started up again. After a low of 14,791 in 1963, it was 15,632 in 1964 and 16,308 in 1965. By 1970 it was 21,811 (although the rise in other breeds was such that the Cocker was No. 12 in popularity). The Cocker continued its new upsweep even as other breeds were falling off. In 1975, the total was 35,492. In 1977 (latest available at this printing) there were 52,955 Cockers registered—fourth highest of all breeds and again the No. 1 of all Sporting dogs. Cocker Spaniel quality has reached a high point as is witnessed by the many beautiful specimens seen not only in the show ring but everywhere one goes.

The long low look of the World War I era as seen in two champions of the time – Ch. Midkiff Creme de la Creme and Ch. Chesasusgue Durbar, owned by Lucknow Kennels.

3

Breed Type

Text and drawings by Ronald B. Fabis

T HERE IS NO DOUBT that spaniels have been in existence for a long time. The "spaniell" out of Spain has been recorded since 1386. Numerous references in print and many interpretations in art have been observed. The first mention of "cocking" spaniels appeared hundreds of years ago and in 1840 the term was used to describe a dog with "a short, round head when compared to that of a springer, much smaller in size, more compact . . . his ears are usually long and well feathered, as are also his legs and tail." No less an authority than James Watson—in 1907—mentions that, contrary to some written opinions, the name "cocking" or cocker spaniel may not necessarily have come from the breed's use for woodcock but rather out of the fact that the term "cock shooting" was commonly used with application to many varieties of game birds including pheasants because the hens were spared to raise up future generations.

The first Cocker Spaniel was registered in the United States in 1879. The American Spaniel Club was founded in 1881, thus predating the Cocker Club in England by four years. Cockers in this country before the turn of the century were of varied type. Standardization did not begin until the advent of Obo II, who was whelped in Canada out of an imported bitch, Chloe II. Some early sources say that his sire Obo was by a Sussex Spaniel out of a Field Spaniel. However James Farrow, who owned him, is quoted as saying that Obo's sire, Bebb—owned by Mr. Bullock—was liver colored. At that time, many people thought that *any* liver dog was a Sussex, but in actuality the dog was bred from the Bullock strain of Cockers, and his dam from a black-and-tan Cocker from Norfolk.

Whatever his lineage, Obo II set a style here that won great appeal and all present show stock has been credited to him. He was criticized in his day for various faults including a tendency to be a "trifle full in the eye," a characteristic which today sets our Cocker apart and gives him his distinctive expression.

Because of the American Kennel Club requirements for three generations of registered stock before a dog can be admitted into its Stud Book, a standard type evolved. This further separated the American and English Cockers since in England, as H. S. Lloyd notes in his book published in 1947, "students of English pedigrees—if they read attentively—will observe that English Springers, other Spaniel varieties, and even Setters have been intermingled with their blood." In this country this interbreeding did not take place, or at least was unrecorded, although dogs did cross the Atlantic both ways and were used interchangeably until the breeds were separated in 1946.

From the 1880s until the late twenties and early thirties the Obo type prevailed—low on leg, long in body, moderate in heads and muzzles and with feathering on the backs of their legs and underside, as illustrated in Figure 1.

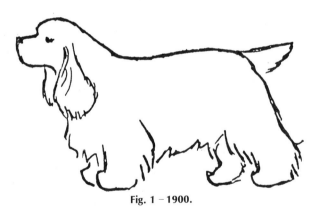

Fig. 1 – 1900.

In the thirties a reappraisal was made by several well-known fanciers and with the use of a few studs of more upstanding type, a "New Look" was created and started to win in the show ring. This type was higher on leg, more compact and with a shorter muzzle, but feathering for the most part was still confined to the back of the legs and underside of the animal. Figure 2 shows the outline which developed. During this era Cockers achieved their greatest popularity.

Fig. 2 – 1935

Our present day show type began to make its appearance in the mid-forties. A few heavy-coated individuals appeared, achieved great success in the ring and were tremendously bred to. This type is characterized by a taller, even more compact animal, with an accentuated stop, higher dome, a shorter deeper muzzle, more slope to the topline, a higher tailset and, of course, greater quantities of feathering—growing all over the leg and body and requiring extensive trimming and shaping to achieve the silhouette in Figure 3.

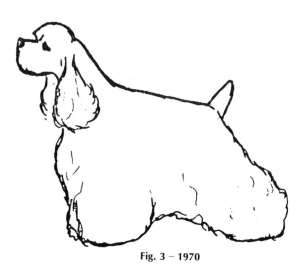

Fig. 3 – 1970

Ch. Denniston Nugget – 1911.

Ch. Lucknow Lothario – 1920.

Ch. The Great My Own – 1930.

Ch. Try Cob's Success–1945.

Ch. Biggs' Believe It Or Not – 1950.

Ch. Biggs' Snow Prince – 1961.

Cocker change through the decades. Each of these was a significant dog of his day. As Mrs. C. B. Maxwell has noted in her fine book "The Truth About Sporting Dogs": "From such as the champion in 1927, much resembling Sussex Spaniel outline, to the highly individual outline of a magnificent show specimen of the 1950s (Believe It Or Not), the change was not merely in terms of the spectacular but also was achieved with surprising speed."

To review some interesting points:

In 1906 and until 1943 the standard required "forelegs *short* and straight," even though Cockers began to be bred higher on the leg by the mid-thirties. In 1957 the standard's description of coat was changed from "well-feathered" to "well-feathered, but not so excessively as to hide the Cocker Spaniel's true lines . . . excessive coat and feathering shall be penalized. " But heavy coats began winning in the mid-forties (and still are). In 1973 the standard was rewritten with particular emphasis on size, coat texture and markings, and all fanciers should be aware of its requirements. (See Chapter 7.) But, as the preceding points illustrate, is the Cocker bred to fit the standard or is the standard changed to fit the dog?

Further, is it too ridiculous to project that in the year 2000 the Cocker may look as in Figure 4?

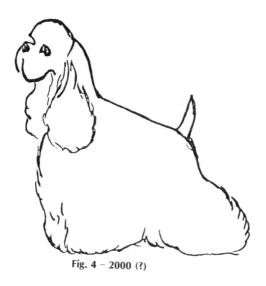

Fig. 4 – 2000 (?)

The Cocker Spaniel has evolved through three major type changes in 70 years. Many breeders and many dogs have influenced these changes. Of course there are still Cockers being bred that resemble the thirties type and there probably always will be, but we are discussing the prevailing show ring representatives.

Today the Cocker is the most popular of all Sporting breeds, and No. 4 of all breeds. The American Spaniel Club has a larger membership

43

and its annual show has more entries than ever before. Certain inherited defects have been diagnosed and proper testing procedures are available to serious breeders.

Where the Cocker will be in 25 years rests in the hands of these breeders and their ability to produce and appreciate a fine dog of proper type. This objective can be cultivated and should remain the main objective of the American Spaniel Club.

Cocker Spaniel
Standard Model

5 in. High
7 in. Long

$2.75 each
Postpaid U.S.A.

Cast in Metal.
Beautifully Plated.
Old Butlers Silver
or
Antique Bronzelite

**A Fine Ornament
for Office, Living
Room or Den**

Modeled to the A. K. C. Standard and approved and indorsed by: The Cocker Spaniel Club of the Midwest, Fred J. Clark of Racine, Wisc., nationally known American Spaniel Club judge; J. A. Blow, Deerfield, Ill., Midwest's largest Cocker Spaniel breeder and A. K. C. judge, and many other Cocker Spaniel breeders and A. K. C. Specialty judges.

A 1938 advertisement that reveals in its own way the changes that have taken place in Cocker Spaniel outline. It would seem that inflation has hit Cocker coats almost as much as it has the price of mail-order items.

"COCKER OF THE YEAR"
The top winners for the years 1960 through 1977

Top winning Cocker Spaniel of 1960 – Ch. Pinetop's Fancy Parade. Parade's record of 28 Bests in Show and 61 Group Firsts for the year topped all dogs of all breeds in the country. He was Best of Breed at the 1961 ASC National Specialty. A black/tan, whelped January 1958, he was bred by Wm. J. Lafoon, Jr., co-owned by Mr. Lafoon and Mrs. Rose Robbins, and handled by Norman Austin.

The top winning Cocker Spaniel of 1961 – Ch. Whitfield's Why Certainly. Winner in the year of 4 Bests in Show and 10 Groups. A son of Ch. Crackerbox Certainly. He was bred by Norman Austin, owned by Mr. and Mrs. William Randall, and handled by Porter Washington.

Top winning Cocker Spaniel of 1962 – Ch. My-Ida-Ho Promise to Maryville. Promise, a parti-color, had 4 Bests in Show, 29 Groups and 3 Specialty Bests of Breed in his career. Bred by Dorothy and Sharon Christiansen (handled by Dorothy), he was owned by Mr. and Mrs. Morris Champers.

Top winning Cocker Spaniel of 1963 and 1964 – Ch. Biggs' Snow Prince. Prince was Best in Show at the 1964 ASC National Specialty, a year in which he won 8 all-breed Bests in Show and 23 Groups. He sired 24 champions. Owned by Jessica Van Ingen and handled by Ted Young.

Top winning Cocker Spaniel of 1965 – Ch. Forjay's Sundown. Winner over a two year span of 12 Bests in Show and 42 Groups. Bred by Mr. and Mrs. Edward Johnston and Phyllis Hulstedt, owned by Dr. William Fritz and handled by Norman Austin.

Top winning Cocker Spaniel of 1966 – Ch. Pinefair Password. Winner in the year of 3 Bests in Show and 12 Groups. A son of Ch. Main-Dale's Mr. Success. Bred and owned by Mrs. H. Terrell Van Ingen and handled by Ted Young.

Top winning Cocker Spaniel of 1967 – Ch. Dream Echo Magic Touch. In a career unfortunately shortened by a leg injury acquired at a dog show, his outstanding wins included the National Specialty in 1968. Owned by Mr. and Mrs. Norman Juelich and handled by the author.

Top winning Cocker Spaniel of 1968 – Ch. Hugomar Headliner, tri-color. Owned by Albert Siekierski's Alco Kennels and handled by Ted Young. Pictured in his win of the 1968 New England Specialty.

49

The top winning Cocker in the nation for 1969 and 1970 – Ch. Burson's Blarney. Bred by Henry Burson and co-owned by Oren Jones and the author's Silver Maple Kennels.

The top winning Cocker Spaniel of all time – Ch. Sagamore Toccoa. Toccoa, Cocker of the Year for 1971 and 1972, was the top winning dog of all breeds in America for 1972. A lovely buff, whelped in 1968, bred by Ted and Lillian Klaiss and owned by Peggy Westphal. Handled by Ted Young.

Top winning Cocker Spaniel of 1973 and 1974 – Ch. Shardeloes Selena. Dam of 6 champions to date. Selena was Best in Show at the ASC National Specialty in both years. Whelped in 1970, she was bred by Lois Hicks-Beach and is owned by Dr. and Mrs. Larry Smith. Shown winning the 1974 Specialty under judge Sunny Dutton with Terry Stacy handling.

Top winning Cocker Spaniel of 1975, Ch. Forjay's Winterwood, winner of 5 Bests in Show, 14 Groups and 7 Bests of Breed. Bred by Edward and Anne Johnston, owned by Donald Robb, and handled by Don Johnston.

The top winning Cocker Spaniel of 1976 and 1977 – Ch. Liz-Bar Magic of Music. In the two year span alone, Magic scored 8 all-breed Bests in Show, 40 Group Firsts and 18 Specialty Bests of Breed. Owned by Mr. and Mrs. Norman Barnes and handled by Don Johnston.

54

4

The Modern
Cocker Spaniel
in America

THE COCKER SPANIEL picture during the past 25 years has been a changing one. Where the earlier dogs were more sparsely coated and with a longer foreface, they now have more profuse coats, shorter muzzles, and are a bit higher on leg with more exaggerated toplines than was seen even a decade ago.

Many kennels that were started during the late forties and fifties are still operating successfully today. It is to these dedicated breeders that much credit must be given. They have been sincere in their efforts to constantly improve the breed and are responsible for many of the beautiful and very sound Cockers we have today.

In the interim, many successful kennels have sprung up and they, too, have contributed a great deal to this progress and deserve much credit. In my endeavor to bring my account of the breed up to date, I will try to mention as many of these dedicated breeders as possible.

Deserving of first place in this catalog of top producing dogs is the great Ch. Scioto Bluff's Sinbad. He holds the all-time top producing record by siring 118 champions. He was bred and owned by Veda and the late Charles Winders and was handled exclusively by Ron Fabis.

In addition to his excellent producing record, Sinbad achieved a fantastic show record. His coloring was dark red and white. You will find a picture and pedigree of Sinbad, as well as those of other outstanding sires and dams, in a special section immediately following this chapter.

55

Also establishing a great record was Orient's Its A Pleasure, owned by Al and Dorothy Orient. Although he was not a champion himself, he sired 101 champions, a truly great record. Thus he became the top non-titled sire in the history of Cocker Spaniels. He was red and white.

Tom O'Neal, to whom the Dreamridge prefix belongs, seemed destined for success as a breeder right from the start. However, his strong affection for the breed began through owning a little red Cocker when he was just 12 years old. He later owned a black and tan but his admiration for the red and whites was responsible for him buying a pretty red and white bitch from the Chuck O'Luck Kennels.

Upon seeing the great Ch. Scioto Bluff's Sinbad, he decided to breed his first parti-colored bitch to him. This breeding produced his first two champions, Ch. Dreamridge Rosie O'Day and Ch. Dreamridge Peter Pan.

Surprisingly enough, the prefix "Dreamridge" was the result of a mistake. Tom contacted Ron Fabis, one of the breed's leading handlers, in regard to showing the two pups. When Ron asked Tom for the registered name of the youngsters, his answer was "Peter and Rosie O'Day." Of course, the handler asked for the prefix or kennel name. Not wishing to admit that his brief experience in breeding had not considered this, Tom saw a sign across the road which read "Green Ridge Cemetery." He immediately replied, "Why, they are called Green Ridge Peter Pan and Green Ridge Rosie O'Day." Ron misunderstood and used "Dreamridge" instead. By the time he learned his error, the two youngsters had earned a number of points. So, the Dreamridge stayed.

Later, Tom acquired two Sinbad daughters, Pounette Perrette from Ed Albers and Cumlaude Marie Elena from Jean Joyce. From that time, his breeding program has been linebreeding through Sinbad, his sons and grandsons, including Ch. Clarkdale Calcutta.

Perrette became the dam of 10 champions, including Ch. Dreamridge Dinner Date, whose nine offspring are all champions. Dinner Date's sister, Dreamridge Double Date, is the dam of 5 champions and the brother Ch. Dreamridge Drambuie, is the sire of 10 champions. Every Cocker in the kennel goes back to Perrette.

Tom has bred 11 Best in Sweepstakes puppies and (in international competition) 4 Best in Show dogs and 11 Group winners. His Ch. Dreamridge Delegate was Best Gundog at the world's largest show, Crufts in London, and was the Top Winning Sporting Dog in England in 1972. Ch. Dreamridge Decorator is a Best in Show recipient in

Ch. Dreamridge Drummer Boy, Ch. Dreamridge Diplomat and Ch. Dreamridge Dandiman with their breeder, Tom O'Neal. Mr. O'Neal was president of the American Spaniel Club in 1976 and 1977.

Ch. Dreamridge Dandiman, red/white, winning Best in Show at the 1975 American Spaniel Club National Specialty under judge Ilmah Newton, with Ron Fabis handling. Owner, Tom O'Neal.

South America. Tom has exported dogs to Canada, Venezuela, Brazil, Argentina, England, Sweden, Holland, Finland and Japan.

Through a wise breeding program and selection, Tom attained the enviable title of Top Breeder of the Year for three consecutive years—1970, '71 and '72.

Though Tom has never become involved in obedience himself, Dreamridge Pink Champagne, owned by the Gilberts of Minneapolis, Minnesota, was the top obedience Cocker in 1973 and one of the ten top obedience Sporting dogs in the Nation. Several others of his breeding have attained CD and CDX degrees.

His most thrilling show win was Best in Show at the American Spaniel Club with Ch. Dreamridge Dandiman in 1975. However, Tom still regards Ch. Dreamridge Dinner Date as the closest to perfection he has attained and, through her son Ch. Dreamridge Dominoe, he is now linebreeding and doubling and tripling on the great Sinbad for more consistent type.

Dominoe is now the top living Cocker Spaniel sire with 80 champion offspring.

The Nor-Mar Kennels of Norman and Mari Doty started, as has been the story with most of our top breeders, with a pet. In 1941, prior to her marriage to Norman, Mari purchased a pet bitch of Stockdale breeding. The bitch was more than Mari really could afford so she bred her to the stud of the breeder's choice, Ch. Judge Bobbie owned by Roy Cowan. She kept a pretty male which she showed, but World War II came along and her activities were set aside for the duration.

In 1947, Mari and Norm were married and as soon as possible they purchased a house on a half-acre. Dogs came soon after. Their main interest was in black and tans, and their first purchase, St. Lo's Sugarfoot was bred to Ch. Sagehill's Bold Venture. From that very first litter came their first champion, Ch. Normar's Nightcap, a brilliantly marked black and tan. Mari handled him for all his points except the last one when, upon getting cold feet, she called on Porter Washington who finished him in one show.

From that first champion to the 48th has been a long way filled with much laughter and many tears. Sugarfoot proved an excellent foundation bitch, however.

Their next purchase was Ch. Pett's Trick or Treat, who had a nice show career. When he was bred to Lois Dubois' daughter of Ch. Biggs' Silver Streak, the only male in the litter proved to be their famous Ch. Nor-Mar's Nujac. This great dog at six months of age placed over five specials at the San Joaquin Valley CSC Specialty. Three months later, at a day or two over nine months, he went Best of Breed from the 9-12 class at the West Coast CSC. He won seven Sporting Groups with Mari handling and in the best of competition.

Their next acquisition was a Medicine Man son out of a Medicine Man daughter, Ch. Kalico's Space Dust, a small, extremely typy black and tan dog. The Dotys considered him a little small for the show ring, but when they did enter him in a local show, he amazed them by going over four specials and then winning the Sporting Group. He finished very quickly with a great record.

In their efforts to continue their line of black and tans, they bred Sugarfoot to Nujac and to their amazement got beautifully marked black and tans. So, they discovered, they had the outcross they were looking for right in their own kennel. The breeding of Nujac and Sugarfoot produced five champions, and Nujac sired 16 champions in all before his early death from cancer.

Newbeetee, from Nujac and Sugarfoot, sired Ch. Nor-Mar's Nockout, another well marked black and tan who did a lot of winning and sired seven champions. His son, Ch. Nor-Mar Nemo was the sire of four champions, including the famous Ch. Nor-Mar's Nautilus.

The purchase of Ch. Smytholms' Beach Boy, a typy black and tan, gave them a needed outcross for their black and tans. Beach Boy sired 17 champions including the outstanding Ch. Nor-Mar's Name of the Game, who has sired nine champions. These two studs are now helping them hold the good type and soundness for which their line is known.

Ch. Main-Dale's Smoke Signal was purchased for the same reason —an outcross. Unfortunately, he is dominantly black. However, his black daughters will carry the black and tan factor for future breedings.

All of their champions have had notable show records along with their excellent producing records. Nujac was the sire of the top winning Ch. Biggs Snow Prince and Ch. Silver Lore of Memoir.

The breeding and showing of the Dotys' dogs is a mutual effort with Mari doing the handling and Norman doing the "behind the scenes" work which is also most important. In addition, Mari edits the *American Cocker Review,* a monthly breed magazine which represents a full time job in itself.

Mark and Dottie Davis have bred champions in three varieties: buffs, tris and black and tans. They have bred 25 champions and are best known for their beautiful buffs. Their Ch. Davis' Dulcinea had an outstanding show record, owner-handled.

Ch. Biggs Honey Dip, purchased in 1952, was the daughter and granddaughter of champion bitches, Honey Dip making the third suc-

Ch. Nor-Mar's Nockout (black/tan- whelped 1964) had a great show record and sired 7 champions.

Ch. Nor-Mar's Nujac (whelped 1957), handsome buff Group winner and sire of 16 champions. Owned by Mari Doty.

Ch. Nor-Mar's Newbeetee, whelped 1958, a distinguished sire. Owned by Norm and Mari Doty.

Ch. Nor-Mar's Name of the Game, b/t whelped 1968, sire of 9 champions.

Ch. Nor-Mar's Nimble-Jac, beautiful cream buff – whelped 1962, a Group winner.

Ch. Nor-Mar's Nautilus, b/t whelped 1970, enjoyed an outstanding show record. Owned by the Dotys.

63

cessive generation. They have two ninth successive generation ASCOB champion bitches in their kennel. A daughter of each is now on the way to championship. They feel this Biggs-Davis bitch line has helped them attain their goal which is to have ten successive generations of champion ASCOB bitches.

More champions have carried the prefix of "Artru" during the past decade than any other kennel name. While they have been very active in breeding since the early fifties, there are a great many of the "Artru" Cockers that have been bred by others. Art and Ruth Benhoff have had the foresight to acquire many fine potentials which have been given the prefix "Artru" and shown to many wins under that name.

Ch. Artru Action, a red male, bred by Dorothy Vanderveer, owned by Bill and Gay Ernst, sired 39 champions.

Ch. Artru Red Baron, bred and owned by Mr. and Mrs. Arthur Benhoff, Jr., another beautiful red, has produced 20 champions to date and is still producing.

Ch. Artru Skyjack, golden buff, bred and owned by the Benhoffs produced 11 champions.

Ch. Artru Available, a red and white, owned by the Benhoffs but bred by Valerie Hitchcock, sired 25 champions and had a Best in Show in '64.

Ch. Artru Johnny Be Good, buff, bred by Bernice and John Muller, was owned and shown by the Benhoffs. He sired 52 champions and was a top producer in 1965, '66, '67, and '69.

Ch. Artru Sandpiper, buff, bred by Corinne Karcher was owned and shown by the Benhoffs. He sired 66 champions, a fabulous record.

Ch. Artru Hot Rod, buff, owned by the Benhoffs and bred by Mrs. Ruth Pusey, had an outstanding show record. He was Best in Show at the National Specialty two years in a row. He was sire of 22 champions.

Ch. Artru Delightful II, a buff bitch, produced 9 champions. She was bred by Marie and Debra Kay Beauchamp and owned by Kathleen M. Lane. Eight of her champions carried the "Artru" prefix.

Ch. Artru Trinket, bred by Fred H. and Virginia Wege and owned by Carol Ann and Toni Mills, finished her title when a year old and half of her wins were from the puppy class. Seven times she was Best Opposite Sex to Best of Variety. She produced 6 champions.

American and Canadian Ch. Bar-C-Kar Peau Rouge, bred and owned by Corinne E. Karcher produced 10 champions—two by Artru Globetrotter and eight by Ch. Artru Johnny Be Good. In 1967, her son Ch. Bar-C-Kar Mr. Chips was Best of Variety over 25 specials at the National Specialty.

Ch. Artru Hot Rod, top winning ASCOB of the late 1950s and the sire of 22 champions. Twice Best in Show at the American Spaniel Club National Specialty. Bred by Mrs. Ruth Pusey and owned by Art and Ruth Benhoff. Handled by Everett Dean.

Ch. Artru Red Baron, sire of 20 champions and still producing. Bred and owned by the Benhoffs.

The expert handling ability of both Ruth and Art Benhoff was responsible for their ability to finish some 25 or 30 champions of their own breeding, in addition to the many bred by others which they were able to acquire. This kennel has contributed a great deal to the improvement in buffs that has been seen during the past 25 years.

The Rexpointe Kennels of Alice Swiderski was started after the arrival of her daughter when she felt she must give up her work with show horses. She fell in love with parti-colors at first sight, and with the help of Marion Bebeau and her son, was fortunate in finding a good one. Her Ch. Rexpointe Captain Holiday was found in short order.

From the start, it was her aim to develop a strain of parti-colors—not just beautiful but sound moving Sporting dogs. Now, after 20 odd years, she feels she is proving her ideas. Sprinkled through the over 40 Rexpointe champions are Best in Show winners, Group winners, a Best in Futurity winner, European Best in Show winners and top producers.

It is her feeling that puppies tend to resemble their total pedigree more often than the immediate sire and dam. The more intensely bred line will dominate.

Ch. Rexpointe Kojak, bred by Alice Swiderski and now owned by Mai Wilson, has had a fantastic career in the show ring, winning Best in Shows and Groups. He is the top winning parti-color in the nation at this writing and is producing well.

Marion Bebeau, of Maribeau fame, grew up on a large farm in Illinois. After she left the farm, her interest in animals continued. When her son Howard became interested, she acquired her first Cocker from Carl Littlejohn, a breeder of that period. Marion's interest increased and it was not long before she acquired a kennel. Her first great win was with Ch. Maribeau March Returns, shown by son Howard to a Best in Show.

Through the years, Maribeau has bred 75 champions. Its top winner and producer is Ch. Maribeau Master Sargent (Bilko) who has produced 36 champions and won the National Specialty in 1965.

Mr. and Mrs. D. LaMar Mathis have had exceptional success in breeding light buff or silver Cockers. Their Ch. LaMar's Ivory Summer was truly a great showgirl and in 1969 was the Top Winning Bitch of the breed. Even after 5 years of age and two litters, she was out winning.

The mating of Ivory Summer to Ch. Artru Johnny Be Good

Ch. LaMar's London, sire of 40 champions. Top producing sire, all varieties, in 1974. A red/white, whelped in 1967, bred and owned by Elaine and D. LaMar Mathis.

Ch. LaMar's Ivory Summer, London's dam. Pictured winning Best in Show at Central Ohio 1969. Ivory Summer was the top winning Cocker bitch of the late '60s. Handled by owner D. LaMar Mathis.

Best In Show

Ch. Rexpointe Kojak, the top winning Parti of 1976 and 1977 with wins in the two years of 3 all-breed Bests in Show, 21 Group Firsts and over 50 other Group placements. A son of Ch. Rexpointe Flying Dutchman, Kojak was bred by Alice Swiderski and is owned by Mai Wilson.

Ch. Rexpointe Flying Dutchman, Best in Show winner and already sire of 15 champions. Bred and owned by Alice Swiderski.

Ch. Rexpointe Shazam, Best of Variety at the summer 1977 ASC National Specialty. Owned by K. L. Marquez.

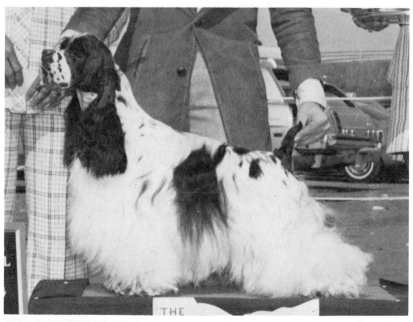

Ch. Rexpointe Reprint winning Best of Breed at the Cocker Spaniel Club of Central Ohio specialty, 1974. A champion-producing sire.

69

produced Ch. LaMar's London, outstanding sire of 40 champion offspring, with more on the way. London was the top producing sire, all varieties, in 1974. His offspring are continuing to produce great show winners. Among his children is Ch. Forjay's Winterwood, the top winning Cocker Spaniel in 1975.

Joanne Thorpe of "Nosowea Cockers" bought her first Cocker for an obedience dog as that was her interest. She was extremely lucky in being able to purchase Scioto Bluff's Spring Romance, half sister of the great Sinbad. Spring Romance obtained her C.D. in two weekends. When Joanne decided to breed her, she was lucky again in her choice, Ch. Camby's Dynamo.

This breeding made history as the great Ch. Nosowea's Spring Nosegay came from this mating. Nosegay was the top winning bitch, all varieties, in 1963. Her show career was outstanding. She finished in two separate weekends at the age of 8 months and 2 days. She won 6 Specialty Bests of Breed, many Varieties and Group placings.

Joanne's greatest producing bitch was Ch. Nosowea's Twice as Nice who was by Ch. Begay's Tan Man. Twice as Nice produced 4 champions out of two litters; her best known was Ch. Nosowea's No Trump. No Trump's many wins included a Best of Variety at the National Specialty in New York. He is also proving a great producer and is back of many of the Nosowea potentials today.

Ch. Scioto Bluff's NosoWayn went overseas to Sweden where he had a Best in Show. He produced four American champions and three Canadian for Nosowea. Nosowea Kennels has bred 26 champions.

The Petts' Kennels was started in 1948 with a black bitch, Pett's Cinderella, with a buff recessive. She was a litter sister of Ch. Elder's So Lovely, dam of Ch. Elderwood Bangaway, a great winner of that time. This was the beginning of what became a most successful career in Cockers.

While their buffs have been better known than the other varieties, they have bred champions in all varieties. Their Ch. Pett's Calendar Girl, a very lovely silver buff sired by Ch. Silver Maple Jimmy Stardust out of Ch. Pett's Bit O'Pamper, was the producer of 6 champions. Her type has carried on through succeeding generations. She produced Ch. Pett's Gentleman Jim, a Best-in-Show dog, and the sire of 16 champions.

Their Ch. Pett's Golden Eagle produced 27 champions and Ch. Pett's Yachtsman produced 17 champions in the Parti-color variety. The Petts' champions are too numerous to list and they are continuing their activities of breeding and finishing top quality Cocker Spaniels.

Ch. Maribeau's Master Sargent, sire of 36 champions. Winner of the 1965 ASC National Specialty. Bred and owned by Marion Bebeau.

Ch. Pett's Daddy's Mink, an outstanding winner of the Roland Petts' kennels.

The Bleuaire Kennels of Patricia L. Blair got its start, as is the story with most beginners, in the school of hard knocks. In the early sixties, through persistence, she acquired a lovely buff bitch from the Palmwood Kennels of Lt. Com. Bert Homan. Bred to a Capital Stock son, the bitch produced her first home-bred champion, Bleuaire's Bewitched. Patricia next acquired a black bitch from the Benwood Kennels of Jess Seidel, which became Ch. Benwood Lady Bleuaire. She finished her championship in less than a month.

Lady Bleuaire produced 5 champions out of two litters sired by Ch. Hob-Nob-Hill's Tribute, as well as another champion by a different stud.

Ch. Sundust Bleubelle, daughter of Ch. Bleuaires Repercussion, was the first American Cocker imported from a foreign country other than Canada to achieve American Championship.

She was bred by Yvonne Knapper of England and owned by Mrs. Blair. She finished her championship quickly with several Bests of Variety, handled by Ron Fabis.

The Bleuaire Kennel has finished 24 champions.

While Hazel and Charles Thompson have been known for many years for their beautiful blacks, their first litter was a parti-color one, sired by Ch. Bar-Nan's Checkers. There was not a champion from this litter, but 7 home-bred parti-color champions came down in later generations from this mating.

Their foundation in blacks was a bitch purchased from Horace Harter of Orchardlawn Kennels. It was not long before this line produced champions. They have bred 35 and 15 of these were sired by their own champions; 29 of the dams were Thompson-bred bitches. The other six came from Ch. DeKarlos Dancing Doll line.

"Doll" was by Ch. Clarkdale Capital Stock and Ch. Thompson's Two-Tone Tersikor, and was sold to the late Karl Schwartz. Due to zoning regulations, she came back to the Thompsons and thus they acquired the famous Dancing Doll. Her show career was terrific and the amazing part was that twice she stopped to have litters and then came back out to win Bests of Breed while her pups were taking wins also. She produced 6 champions.

Their Suntan Sue produced 6 champions, all blacks, though they had hoped through Sue, to get some top buffs. Her top producer was Ch. Thompson's Town Traveler, acquired by us when quite young. He produced 18 champions for our Silver Maple Kennels.

The Golden Acre Kennels of Nancy Block is built on determination, vision and a lot of hard work. At the age of eleven, Nancy acquired her

72

Ch. Nosowea's No Trump, Best of Variety at the 1971 National Specialty of the American Spaniel Club. Bred and owned by Joanne Thorpe.

Ch. Bleuaire's Persistence, one of the many Bleuaire champions bred by Patricia L. Blair.

73

Ch. Biggs' Snow Flurry being handled to Best in Show win from the Open class by Norman Austin. Bred and owned by Mr. and Mrs. Robert W. Biggs.

Ch. DeKarlos Dancing Doll had an outstanding show career and was dam of 6 champions. Owned by Charles and Hazel Thompson.

Ch. Sagamore Golden Rhythm, sire of 17 champions. Owned by Nancy Block's Golden Acre Kennels.

Ch. Golden Acre's Orange Pekoe, a top winning Cocker of the Southeast in the '70s with 54 BOVs. Owned and shown by Bowman Davis, Glen Hill Kennels.

first Cocker for the $40 she had carefully saved over a period of time. She soon learned that it was not a show dog.

She persevered, constantly learning, until when she graduated from high school she was able to purchase a good bitch. The dog was sent to a handler, but unfortunately a week later was killed by a car. She was then able to buy a half sister, Essanar Eastwind, who finished very quickly and produced two champions from her first litter.

Later Nancy acquired a young male, Sagamore Golden Rhythm, at 4 months of age. He earned his championship very quickly and has proven a great producer for her and for others. He is the sire of 17 champions.

Nancy's Ch. Sagamore Sprite had a great show record with 3 Group Firsts and many other Group placings and 45 Bests of Variety.

The Dur-Bet Kennels of Elizabeth H. Durland began breeding seriously in 1959 and since that time 40 homebreds have finished their championships. This kennel has been most fortunate in producing bitches. Their Ch. Dur-Bet's Nightie Night produced 4 champions including the two famous brothers, Ch. Dur-Bet's Knight to Remember and American and Canadian Ch. Dur-Bet's Pick the Tiger.

Their Ch. Dur-Bet's Leading Lady is the dam of 9 champions. Ch. Jo-Be-Glen's Maria produced 6 champions. These three, along with Ch. Dur-Bet's Tantilizer, have fashioned the Dur-Bet Cockers of today.

Ch. Dur-Bet's Knight to Remember had an outstanding show career, having won Best of Breed at the National Specialty in 1969 and '71. He produced 24 champions and Pick the Tiger produced 15 champions.

Mrs. Durland has been a very active person in obedience work and has had connections with many other organizations associated with animals. She has a background in zoology and medical research and works hard for programs to minimize crippling defects in order to secure the future of the breed. She is a member of the American Spaniel Club's committee to study hereditary and congenital defects and Chairman for the Health Registry Sub-Committee.

The Biggs' name is one that has been known since 1938 and theirs is one of the few kennels that have bred continuously since the '30s, breeding champions through the years.

During this period they have owned scores of champions, either bred by them or chosen from litters sired by their champions. Their first great champion was Biggs' Cover Charge who sired 18 champions.

Ch. Dur-Bet's Knight to Remember, Best of Breed at the American Spaniel Club National Specialty in 1969 and 1971, and sire of 24 champions. Bred and owned by Elizabeth H. Durland and handled by Tom Campbell.

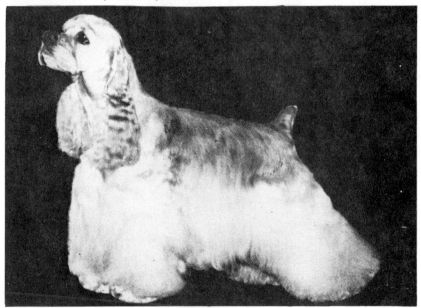

Am. & Can. Ch. Bobwin's Boy Eagle, whelped 1972, has sired 15 champions. Bred and owned by Winnie Vick.

Ch. Har-Dee's Heartbeat produced 7 champions. Owned by the Schultzes' Har-Dee Kennels.

Am. & Can. Ch. Har-Dee High Spirit, sire of 17 champions. Black/tan, whelped 1968. Owned by Harold and Delphie Schultz.

78

His sire was Ch. Eash's Golden Boy, also a great producer, siring 12 champions himself.

Their "Snow" dogs, Snow Flurry and Snow Prince, were spectacular showmen. Ch. Biggs' Snow Flurry had a great career with one Best in Show, but it was Ch. Biggs' Snow Prince who was the real sensation. He produced 29 champions, had 8 Bests in Show and placed number one in Sporting dogs in '65. Snow Prince was later sold to Jessica Van Ingen of Pinefair fame. Ted Young continued to show him and he spent his remaining days at the Tedwin Kennels.

Carol and Bob Biggs were great travelers and visited Cocker folks in many foreign countries. Their Ch. Biggs' Gay Cavalier had a great record in France with the Firminacs, his owners. When visiting in Japan, they were treated royally by the Cocker Club who postponed their specialty so they might attend.

The Pryority Kennels of Bill and Marilyn Pryor really started in 1965 although a Cocker pet had always been a member of their household. After searching for a replacement of a lost pet, they began to realize there was a difference between show dogs and just pets.

With the help of several knowledgeable breeders, they were able to obtain a sound foundation bitch, Merrydown Merry Christmas. When bred to Ch. Valli-Lo's Viceroy, a Capital Stock son, she gave them many champions bearing the Pryority prefix. Ten champions were finished, and many had fantastic records in foreign countries.

Presentation, when he finished his American championship, was sold to Mr. and Mrs. Robert Marx-Nielson of Cascais, Portugal. On November 23, 1968, in Amsterdam, Holland, he defeated 2310 dogs at the Royal Holland Kennel Club Winners Show to become Reserve Best in Show in his European debut.

Ch. Pryority Parisienne was the dam of 4 champions. Her litter by Ch. Laynewood Lancer was very productive. A black and tan went to Yvette Kapferer in France where he became Int. and Fr. Ch. Pryority's Passport. Another black and tan, named Pryority Patroon, went to Will deVriss-Hoogland in Holland.

Ch. Pryority Patriot, from this same litter, handled usually by Ron Fabis, had a fabulous career in the show ring placing number three black Cocker in the nation in 1973, with a Best in Show to his credit. In 1975, he placed fifth in the Nation among top winning Cockers.

Ch. Pryority Pioneer, from a repeat of the mating that produced Patriot, was sold to the Golden Gate Kennels of Sonja and Ricardo Kohn of Rio de

Janeiro, Brazil. In 1976, Pioneer completed his International and Brazilian Championships, as well as winning two all-breed Bests in Show.

With the Best in Show win of International Champion Pryority's Passport at Bouafles, France, in June of 1976. Pryority has produced Best in Show dogs on three continents.

The Clarkdale Kennels of Leslie and the late Elizabeth Clark was founded through a stroke of luck. They were able to acquire the dam of their foundation bitch, Van Valzah's Viking Girl, indirectly through Mrs. Helen Considine. Bred to Van Valzah's King of Hearts, Viking Girl gave them Ch. Clarkdale Candy and Cake, the foundation of their parti line.

Ch. Clarkdale Capital Stock became their greatest black, both in the show ring and as a producer. A true immortal, he won 17 all-breed Bests in Show and 25 Bests of Breed in specialty shows. He was even greater as a producer, siring 76 champions. His dam, Ch. Clarkdale Closing Quotation, daughter of the great Ch. Elderwood Bangaway, also proved a great producer.

In parti-colors, Ch. Clarkdale Calcutta had a great show record, as did Ch. Clarkdale Chicadee.

Delphie Schultz and her late husband, Harold, have been dedicated breeders for many years. Their Ch. Har-Dee High Spirit sired 18 champions. Their Har-Dee's Heartbeat produced 7 champions. They were also the breeders of Ch. Har-Dee's Hell Bender II, owned by the Robin Knoll Kennels who had a good show career. Delphie is still carrying on and breeding show winners.

The Shardeloes Kennels, of Lois Hicks-Beach, has the distinction of being the breeder of a truly great bitch, Ch. Shardeloes Selena. She was purchased by Dr. and Mrs. Larry Smith and campaigned by them to a wonderful career topped with two successive Best in Show wins at the National Specialty. She has produced 6 champions to date.

Since Lois started breeding seriously in 1960, she has produced several outstanding show winners. Her first champion, Smytholm's Good Grief, a black and tan, bred to Ch. Magicours Monogram, produced 2 champions in the first litter. One was Ch. Smytholm's Beach Boy, a Best in Show and multi-Group winner.

The pages of history will record the name of Ch. Shardeloes Selena along with Ch. Idahurst Belle II, as being the only two Cocker bitches to take consecutive top wins at the American Spaniel Club's top specialty. Ch. Idahurst Belle II was Best in Show there in 1930, '31

Ch. Clarkdale Calcutta had a great show record.

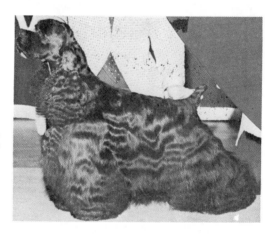

Ch. Pryority's Patriot, Best in Show winner — number 3 Cocker in the nation for 1973. Bred and owned by Marilyn Pryor.

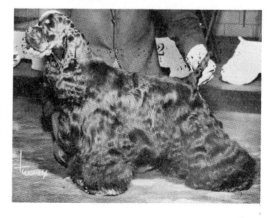

Ch. Pryority's Presentation, bred by Marilyn Pryor and sold to Mr. and Mrs. Robert Marx-Nielson of Cascais, Portugal.

81

and '32, and Selena was Best in Show in 1973 and 1974. Terry and Charlotte Stacy were her handlers during her entire career.

Dorothy and Sharon Christiansen of My-Ida-Ho Kennels of the Pacific Northwest, have had the distinction of showing two parti-colors to outstanding records. Ch. My-Ida-Ho Promise to Maryville was retired in November of 1962 with a Best in Show, his fourth. He also had 29 Groups, 2 Bests of Breed, and many Varieties and Group placings. Sold at an early age to Mr. and Mrs. Morris Champers of Maryville, Washington, Promise was shown exclusively by Dorothy.

Another great dog shown by Dorothy and Sharon was Ch. Stonewalk Squareshooter purchased from Ron Fabis when just a year of age. He was the top winning Cocker of all varieties in the Northwest for six years. He sired 18 champions and his show record was terrific—3 Bests in Show, 30 Groups and 4 Bests of Breed. This included some wins in Canada.

The Kobbytown Kennels of Norma and Anthony Donderwitz started as have many kennels with a gift puppy, just a pet. She remained their house pet but they soon realized they must look further for quality. Their early showing was mostly in Canada as these shows were much closer to their location, and they did considerable winning there.

I had the pleasure of finishing their first American Champion, Kobbytown Cappie, and also their Ch. Kobbytown's Liberty Love. Their Ch. Leelon's On Parade, a black and tan, had a great career in Canada with several Bests in Show, Groups and Specialty Show wins.

Their Am. and Canadian Ch. Magicours Monitor, purchased from Richard Thomas, was awarded Top Sporting Dog of Canada in 1966. Their latest champion, Kobbytown's High Honor, was specialed in both countries. This dog has had a tremendous show record and is proving a great producer.

The Campbell Cocker Kennels was established seriously in 1965 with the purchase of a tri-color male from the Merlady Kennel. As with so many, he was originally purchased as a pet. After joining the Cocker Club, the Campbells were encouraged to show him. He became Ch. Merlady's Rhetorical Romeo and is still living at 12 years of age.

This was the start of what has become a very interesting and active hobby for the Campbells. They have bred and owned many champions. Many of their dogs have been registered with the name Campbell's Color Me Something, which has certainly distinguished their names from the ordinary.

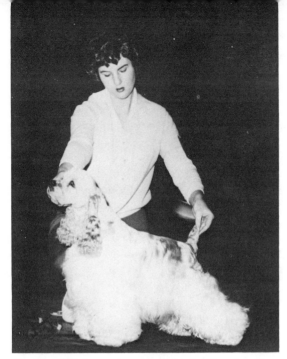

Ch. Stonewalk Squareshooter (whelped 1962), sire of 18 champions. Squareshooter was the top winning Cocker in the Northwest for six years and won 3 Bests in Show. Bred by Ron Fabis, and owned by Dorothy and Sharon (pictured) Christiansen.

Ch. Kobbytown's High Honor, Best of Breed at the 1974 Upstate Cocker Club Specialty. Owned by Norma and Anthony Donderwitz.

Their Ch. Campbell's Court Queen won the National Futurity in 1975. Her dam, Ch. Campbell's Color Me Cute, produced 6 champions. One of her daughters, Ch. Campbell's Color Me Quaint, is the dam of the 1975 Futurity Winner.

The Sandrex Kennels of Jim and Donna Pfrommer is not an old kennel, but it has been a productive one. Jim has loved Cockers and all dogs for many years, but Donna had a great fear of all dogs due to an attack by a dog when she was just a young girl. It took great courage to finally overcome this fear and achieve her goal.

The Pfrommers were fortunate in securing some stock from the Essanar Kennels, a kennel which eventually disbanded. At that time, they acquired Ch. Essanar Eastside, now the sire of some 27 champions. The Pfrommers are idealistic in their approach to perfection in Cockers.

Ch. Essanar Evening Song, bred by Hansi Rowland and Mildred Seger, and owned by the Pfrommers was dam of 9 champions.

As with most breeders of today, Laura and Kap Henson purchased a pet for their children of show quality. When she was four years old, they decided to breed her once. They were referred to the Pfrommers and she was bred to Ch. Essanar Eastside. There were six puppies and three were show quality. Two of these were finished by the Pfrommers, Ch. Sandrex Sarsaparilla and Ch. Sandrex Steinsong. The third, a red bitch, was kept by the Hensons and became their top producer.

Sangarita was bred at 4 years of age to Ch. Lurola Royal Lancer. A total of 7 champions came from this same breeding and two more champions came from their own Ch. Kaplar's Butch Cassidy.

Ch. Kaplar's Royal Kavalier is now owned by Jack Hull and he is being campaigned extensively.

In their second litter, there were three Best of Breed winners. Ch. Kaplar's Royal Kavalier was Top Winning ASCOB for '76, and Ch. Kaplar's Kopi-Kat was Top Winning ASCOB Bitch for 1976. Kavalier was Best in Show at the National Specialty in 1977.

Wilbert Helmick has been interested in Cockers for many years, and produced some good ones in the past. However, it is only in the last few years that he has had the time to devote to his hobby and it has paid off. With the purchase of Ch. Golden Acres Up, Up and Away, a bitch I had the pleasure of finishing and then acquired and later sold to him, he has had remarkable success.

She has produced 7 champions for him and an offspring has

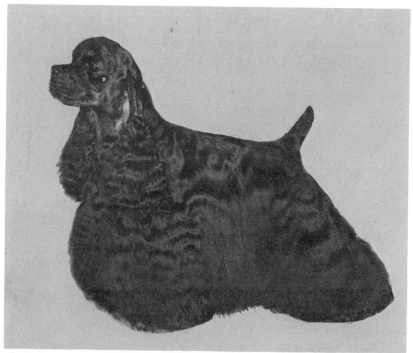

Ch. Kaplar's Royal Kavalier, top winning ASCOB in the nation for 1976 and 1977. Best in Show at the 1977 American Spaniel Club National Specialty. Bred by Kap and Laura Henson, he has recently been purchased by Jack Hull.

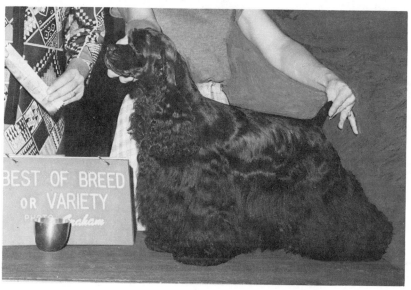

Ch. Kaplar's Koka Kola, Best of Breed at the Maryland Cocker Spaniel Club Specialty, 1975 under judge Mrs. James E. Clark. Bred and owned by Kap and Laura Henson (handler).

Am. & Can. Ch. Seven Acres Spatter Paint, whelped 1964, one of 31 champions bred by Martha Jean Robinson.

Ch. Seven Acres Skyrocket, also owned by Martha Jean Robinson.

Ch. Stonewalk Sharpshooter, sire of 14 champions. Red/white, whelped 1960. Bred by Ron Fabis, and owned by Jean W. Van Patten's Twyneff Kennels.

h. Wib's Society Rose had a great show record. Bred and owned by Wilbert Helmick.

Ch. Golden Acre's Up, Up and Away, dam of 8 champions. Owned by Wilbert Helmick.

Earnscliffe Erving, whelped 4. Owned by Ruth and Dick mgartner, who have finished 8 mpions.

produced one. The greatest, Up, Up and Away's daughter, Ch. Wib's Society Rose, has had a remarkable show record.

The Seven Acres Kennels of Martha Jean Robinson has been the breeder of 31 champions. Her greatest producers were: Ch. Seven Acres Sunshine, dam of 7 champions, and the stud, Ch. Seven Acres Sun Beau, sire of 7 champions. All seven of the Ch. Seven Acres Sunshine champions were sired by Ch. Arco Arnie. Her greatest show winner was Am. and Can. Ch. Seven Acres Spatter Paint.

The Charberson Kennels of Milford K. and Bernice Stimpson Toney were not in operation too long, but had a remarkable record during approximately six years. During this time, they finished 9 champions, 6 of which were homebred.

Their Ch. Charberson's Mistletoe was top winning black bitch in 1963 although shown only six months. She was top winning bitch all varieties in 1964, also shown only six months. Her one litter produced three females, two of which finished their championships.

Ruth and Dick Baumgartner of Earnscliffe Cockers have been concentrated on blacks in their breeding. Their first homebred, Ch. Earnscliffe Status Seeker, produced 9 champions. His son, Ch. Earnscliffe Executive, finished while still a puppy, winning sweepstakes and 3 Bests in Show in Bermuda, and was a Top Ten winner in 1969. They have finished 8 Earnscliffe champions, all black.

The Plantation Kennels owned by Betty Schachner, her mother Minerva Purcell, and daughter Lisa, has been in operation since the early '50s. They have finished 28 champions by various studs.

They have been fortunate in Futurity wins at the National Specialty. The first win was in 1956 when Plantation's Little Lou went up. In 1969, their Plantation's Easter Bonnet was the winner. In 1975, Artru Jericho won the ASCOB honors. All went on to championships.

They have been very active in their local school system, giving programs during the school term featuring purebred dogs. They are also to be commended for their work with 4-H girls and boys in judging and training at the Country Fairs; also with the Girl and Boy Scout groups.

The "Gina's" Cockers of Dolores Roca have come a long way through her hard work and devotion to the breed. She has bred 19 champions and has developed a line that is continuing to produce type and quality. Her beautiful black bitch, Ch. Gina's Midnight Minx,

Ch. Valli-Lo's Flash Away, black, whelped. Finished to championship as a puppy, he became sire of 31 champions. Bred and owned by Mrs. John Brojanac.

h. Cameo's Dawn Friar Tuck, the p winning black Cocker Spaniel r 1976 and sire of 17 champions. ed by Mrs. John Brojanac and vned by Mrs. Beth Speich.

89

Ch. Campbell's Color Me Cute, CD, dam of 6 champions. Her daughter, Ch. Campbell's Court Queen won the National Futurity in 1975. Owner, H. W. Campbell.

Ch. Charberson's Mistletoe, a top winning bitch in the 1960s. Owned by Milford K. and Bernice Toney.

Ch. Artru Jan-Myr Camelot, one of the top current ASCOBs, pictured in Best in Show win under judge Wm. Fetner. Owned by Otto and Marie Walzel, Loch Lane Kennels, and handled by Mr. Walzel.

Ch. Artru Jericho, the ASCOB Futurity winner of the 1975 National Specialty. Owned by Betty Schachner, her mother Minerva Purcell, and her daughter, Lisa (handling).

91

produced 5 champions and has left her mark on her offspring through four generations. Her latest Ch. Gina's Creampuff Maker finished in five straight shows, all big shows including the National Specialty.

Ch. Cameo's Dawn Friar Tuck, owned by Mrs. Beth Speich and bred by Mrs. John Brojanac, is the sire of 17 champions. His son, Ch. Champagne's Dynamic, who is currently being campaigned and has sired 10 champions, is his greatest producing offspring. Friar Tuck was top winning black for 1976.

Ch. Deep River Dazzle, a very flashy parti-color and the sire of 20 champions, was bred by Mrs. James Scofield. Owned and shown for some time by Pat and Lee Wendleton, he has just recently been sold to Ken and Dorothy Lindsey and will continue to be at stud with them.

The Twyneff Kennels of Jean W. Van Patten has been in existence since the early 1950s. Most of the champions she has finished have been owner-handled. She acquired Ch. Stonewalk Sharpshooter in the '60s from his breeder, Ron Fabis and he sired 14 champions. She acquired Ch. Marpet Beach Comber from Marion Peterson in the '70s and he sired 12 champions for her and is still producing.

The Loch Lane Kennels of Otto and Marie Walzel began about 1952 after they attended their first big show, the American Spaniel Club's Zone Specialty held at the Shamrock Hotel in Houston, Texas. There was an all-time record entry of 295, with three rings being judged at the same time. Their win of Best Local over 40 entries was all it took to sell them on the fun of showing Cockers. From then on, there were wins and disappointments as was to be expected, but they have stayed in there pitching with much success.
Their Ch. Loch Lane Yogolita had a nice specials career. Their greatest wins have been with Ch. Candylane Cosmopolitan, purchased from Dick and Betty Duding. He has sired 20 champions and had a great specials career.

Mr. and Mrs. Walter Thompson of Butch Kennels have accomplished a great deal in the short time they have been interested in show Cockers. They started out in 1969 with their first—yes, they thought it was a show Cocker.
The next two years were full of trials and tribulations. They were fortunate in acquiring a good bitch from David Lowe, Ch. Ca-Da's Bikini. She became an excellent foundation bitch and produced 4 of the 8 champions they have bred.

92

David John Lowe's Ca-Da Cockers have produced 27 champions. Ch. Ca-Da's Bikini became the foundation bitch of Walter and Rachel Thompson's Butch Kennels.

Ch. Artru Patent Leather, an excellent show dog that has proved himself as a topnotch hunting dog. A Best in Show and Specialty winner with many Group Firsts, he was one of the top three Blacks of 1976. Owned by Walter D. and Rachel Thompson's Butch Kennels.

The top champion they have owned is Ch. Artru Patent Leather. He was a Best in Show dog and the top Black Cocker in 1975. They have found this a wonderful avocation and I feel the Thompsons will be "in" Cockers for many years to come. They have acquired 15 champions since 1972.

David John Lowe of Ca-Da Cockers, has produced 27 champions. His Ch. Ca-Da's Plum Brandy produced 6 champions. Ch. Van Valzah's Vintage produced 15 champions.

The Juniper Kennels of Ina S. Ginsberg has bred 21 champions. Ch. Juniper Jamaica produced 7 champions, all sired by Ch. Hob-Nob-Hill Hob-Nobber. Her top winning male was Ch. Juniper Jambora.

Juniper Juliette, a buff female, produced 5 champions, all sired by Ch. Biggs' Snow Prince. Another son, Ch. Juniper Just Snowed, was the sire of the 1967 Futurity Winner.

The Forjay Kennel was started in the late fifties or early sixties by the late Ed and Anne Johnston. The Forjay name came about because "J" was the first letter of their name and with their two boys, there were four of them.

They were particularly interested in black and tans. In 1960, they were able to lease Creedaire Miss Moccasin from Phyllis Hulstead St. John, a bitch of St. Andrea's Medicine Man and Ch. Elderwood Bangaway breeding.

This breeding nicked and their great Ch. Forjay's Sundown came from this mating. He was sold to Dr. William Fritz and was campaigned under his name. Sundown's show record under the handling of Norman Austin included: 12 Bests in Show, 47 Group firsts, 18 Group seconds, 11 Group thirds and 11 Group fourths. He won 10 Bests of Breed and 141 Bests of Variety. Upon his retirement, he was returned to Forjay to live out his lifespan.

Sundown's great grandson, Ch. Forjay Winterwood, was top Cocker of the year and number 6 Top Sporting Dog in 1975. He had 5 Bests in Show, 14 Group firsts and 7 Bests of Breed. He was handled by Donald Johnston, son of Ed and Anne, who is continuing the breeding operation of the Forjay Kennels.

The Candylane Kennels of Dick and Betty Duding had its start about 19 years ago in St. Louis, Missouri, where, with some cooperation from Lee and me, they became deeply involved in the fascinating hobby of breeding and showing Cocker Spaniels. Because of Dick's

Ch. Juniper Jamaica, dam of 7 champions. One of 31 champions bred by the Juniper Kennels of Ina S. Ginsberg.

Ch. Deep River Dazzle, parti-color, sire of 20 champions. Bred by Mrs. James Scofield and now owned by Ken and Dorothy Lindsey.

Ch. Gina's Creampuff Maker, Winners Bitch at the National Specialty in 1977. Finished to championship in five straight shows. Owned by Dolores Roca.

95

business connections, they made many moves in the next few years, but their interest in Cockers never waned.

They have finished around 50 champions of which 37 were homebred. Their top producers were Ch. Candylane Cosmopolitan with 22 champions and Ch. Candylane Cadet with 12. Their top producing bitches were Ch. Candylane Coquette with 9 champions and Ch. Harlanhaven Helter Skelter with eight. Both of these are on the all-time producing bitch list.

They feel that Coquette has done more for parti breeding than any other individual they have owned. She had a beautiful head, proper coat texture, excellent conformation and a lovely temperament.

The Breezy Hill Kennels of Paul C. and Anita Hipsley purchased its first Cocker in 1944. Through selective breeding there have been many Breeze Along champions since that time. Their foundation was Ch. Breeze Hill Breeze Along who was also a great showman.

The Robin Knoll Kennels of Norma Krumwiede and Jack Schaffter has been in operation during the past decade. During that period they have produced 21 champions. Their Ch. Robin Knoll Hell Bender had a great show record and was a great producer.

Jean and Bill Peterson of the Rinky Dink Kennels, started as so many have with an interest in obedience, some 12 years ago. As they watched the conformation classes at the shows, they became more and more impressed with the beauty of the show dogs. So, they just had to have one and were lucky in buying a black and tan, Rinky Dink's Shadow. The thrill they knew when he finished sold them on the fun a show Cocker can bring.

Their purchase of Robin, later to be Ch. Rinky Dink's Robin, was a lucky one. Robin was bred by Eugene Skweres. She has produced 7 champions for the Petersons and these champions are now proving producers.

Their Ch. Rinky Dink's Sir Lancelot has proven a great specials dog and is greatly sought after for stud service. His record of producing should reach great heights. He has produced many champions to date and is continuing to produce winners.

Mrs. Muriel R. Laubach was breeder-owner of Ch. Dauhan's Justin Morgan, the sire of 25 champions. He was never specialed as was his sire, Ch. Dauhan Dan Morgan, who had a beautiful show record. Dan won 69 Bests of Variety, 23 Groups and 3 All-Breed Bests in Show.

Ch. Candylane Coquette, dam of 9 champions. Candylane Kennels is owned by Dick and Betty Duding.

Ch. Silver Maple Windfall, whelped 1971, producing well for the Mari-Ken Kennels of Marilyn and Ken Douglas.

The Hob-Nob-Hill Kennels of Kay and Larry Hardy started with the purchase of a pet Cocker when they resided on the "Hill" in San Francisco. Their attachment for this location was the reason for the name they gave their kennel.

After moving to New England, they became serious about their breeding and, with the help of others, were soon on their way. Their foundation bitch was Saucebox, a sister of Ch. Hob-Nob-Hill's Hifalutin' and her bitch line has consistently produced champions for the Hardys.

Their greatest producers were Ch. Hob-Nob-Hill Hob-Nobber, who produced 12 champions, and Ch. Hob-Nob-Hill Tribute, who was sold to Dr. Clarence A. Smith, and produced 54 champions.

Heyday Kennels, owned by Clarence A. Smith, now of Chapel Hill, N. C., was granted the right to this name in 1948. Before this time, two champions had been finished, the first Ch. High Hampton Jessamine, the second Ch. Covered Brook Cinders, and home-bred Cockers had been shown at local shows. The first champion finished under the Heyday prefix was Heyday Glory Be, which was to be the first of many black bitches owned by Dr. Smith. Since that date, 1949, 43 champions have worn the Heyday name.

Frequent transfers as a career officer in the U.S. Public Health Service made 11 different locations in the South and Mid-West the home address. Obviously, this kind of life limited a sustained breeding program, as did five years of apartment living.

Larry Smith has concentrated since 1950 on high quality black and black and tan breeding, but not until 1965, when he acquired the young black Ch. Hob Nob Hill's Tribute, did he enter into specials competition on a serious basis. "Nicky," shown by the Stacys, had an outstanding record. Shown in 1965 through 1967, he had 10 Bests of Breed in Specialties, a Best in Show at Columbus, Ga. (1966) and won 10 Sporting groups. He produced 54 champions, black or black and tan.

Next came the black and tan dog, Ch. Heyday Hobbit, the first Heyday homebred to win Best in Show and Specialty honors. Hobbit won 2 Bests in Show, 12 Bests of Breed, and over 30 Group placings. He was the top ASCOB winner in 1968 and was the sire of 9 champions before his death in 1974.

Their next great was Ch. Heyday Henrietta, a black bitch who produced 7 champions and was a top winner for over two years.

Ch. Shardeloes Selena was the next great one to be owned by Dr. Smith, and her fabulous career is accounted elsewhere in this book.

Ch. Hob-Nob-Hill Hobnobber, whelped 1962, homebred sire of 32 champions for the Hob-Nob-Hill Kennels of Kay and Larry Hardy.

Ch. Heyday Hobbit, black/tan whelped in 1966, the first homebred of Dr. and Mrs. Clarence Smith's Heyday Kennels, had a fine record including two Bests in Show and Specialty wins.

Eight of her offspring have become champions and two of her sons are Best of Breed winners, one a Best in Show winner.

Dr. Smith has retired but he continues in the hobby that has brought him such pleasure for over 30 years.

The Jersie Hill Kennels of Gene and Lois Kistner has certainly made great headway in quality and type. While their record only shows 5 champions and another co-owned, many of their promising bitches have been sold and the new owners encouraged to finish. Their Ch. Jersie Hills Hometown Dust has produced 5 champions.

On July 5, 1975, Seenar's Sinful completed his championship and this established a new producing record for his dam, Ch. Seenar's Seductress. The previous record, which had stood for 22 years, had been held by Ch. Honey Creek Vivacious with 14 champions. This record of 15 champions for Seductress, bred and owned by Ramona and Carl Cantrell, should stand for many years.

The Van-Dor Kennels of Dorothy Vanderveer was a great influence on reds and buffs during the late '60s and '70s, prior to her death in 1975. She was the breeder of top producing Ch. Artru Action, who has produced close to 50 champions to date.

Dr. Carl Oldham, besides being a very successful veterinarian, has enjoyed the hobby of raising some top winning Cocker Spaniels, and helping others as he went along. His Ch. Main-Dale's Mr. Success produced 46 champions. His Ch. Main-Dale's Golden Touch had a very fine show career winning Groups and a Best in Show. Another fine dog bred by Dr. Oldham is Ch. Main-Dale's Smoke Signal, now owned by Norman and Mari Doty and building a very fine record on the West Coast.

Ch. Dream Echo Magic Touch, though owned by Mr. and Mrs. Norman Juelich, was whelped at our Silver Maple Kennels and spent practically all of his short life there. He sailed through to his championship in short order and then proceded to make a great name for himself, becoming the top winning Cocker in the Nation in 1968, a year in which he also won the National Specialty.

His career was shortened at its height by an injury to his leg which happened at a dog show. It also shortened his life, as he only lived to the age of 7 years. However, during that time, he was able to sire 27 champions.

Ch. Heyday Henchman, Dr. Smith's newest Specials dog, the No. 2 black Cocker in the nation for 1977 with an all-breeds Best in Show, 2 Specialties, and 5 Group Firsts.

Ch. Heyday Henrietta, whelped 1969, produced 7 champions and was a top winner for over two years. Owned by Dr. and Mrs. Clarence A. Smith.

Ch. Silver Maple Sharp Tri-Umph, whelped in 1962, sire of 17 champions. Bred and owned by the author's Silver Maple Kennels.

Ch. Thompson's Town Traveler (whelped 1968), sire of 19 champions. Bred by Mrs. Hazel Thompson and acquired at an early age by Silver Maple Kennels.

Ch. Silver Maple Top Hat 'N Tails.

Ch. Silver Maple Lamplighter, owned by Don and Sue Groves, is producing well.

103

Ch. Magicour's Monogram was bred and owned by Richard Thomas. In 1965, he was the top producing ASCOB. He finished his championship at 9 months with 4 majors. He was the sire of 24 champions.

The Birchwood Kennels, owned by Ed McCauley and Don Harrison, has been breeding and showing some top winners in recent years. Their late Ch. Birchwood Bacharack was their most influential sire. Their top producing bitch was Ch. Birchwood Bardot. Their top winner was Cindy Mueller's Bric-a-Brac.

Ch. Glen Hollow Standout was bred and is owned by Paul and Diane Lizotte. They became interested in breeding Cockers in the late '60s and laid a foundation on Ch. Silver Maple Party Favor. Her producing record of 8 champions gave them an excellent start in the breed. They have finished 15 champions.

Ch. Fi-Fo Fiesta was bred by Marty L. Reed and owned by Mrs. Eunice G. Reed. She produced 11 champions, all sired by Ch. Pett's Yachtsman. Fiesta was a tri-color.

Our own Silver Maple Kennels has been in existence since 1936. During these four decades, we have bred over 60 champions, and have finished many more sired by our champions.
Our Ch. Silver Maple Sharp Tri-Umph, a tri-color, sired 17 champions. Our Ch. Thompson's Town Traveler, which we purchased at an early age, has sired 19 champions. Some of our bitches have done well too. Ch. Silver Maple Party Favor produced 8 champions and Ch. Silver Maple Barbie Kay produced 5 champions.
Ch. Burson's Blarney, which we co-owned and handled, was top Cocker in the nation during 1969 and 1970.
Ch. Silver Maple Lamplighter, owned by Don and Sue Groves, and bred by Silver Maple Kennels, is proving a good producer.

The Trojan Kennels of Alice Kaplan has been in operation many years and most of her wins have been owner-handled. She has had great success with solid-parti breeding.
There have been 21 champions finished under the Trojan prefix. She was breeder of the parti sire Ch. Trojan Tagalong, sire of 10 champions. Her top producing bitch was Ch. Trojan Tangelic, which produced 6 champions.

The Marley Kennels of Mildred Marvin and Edna Riley produced a

Ch. Laurim's Command Performance, red/white whelped 1967, sire of 15 champions. Owned by Laurabeth and Dr. James R. Duncan.

Ch. Briarhaven Bourbon Baron, black/tan whelped 1970, sire of 15 champions. Owned by Jack Hull.

top winner in the early sixties. Their Ch. Marley's Brookwood Rumpus was the South's top winning ASCOB and number 5 in the nation. They are continuing to breed champions and their latest is Ch. Marley's Miss Hilarity.

The late Natalie Maas bred 6 champions and co-bred 5 or 6 more. She purchased and completed the championship of many more. Perhaps the greatest of these from a producing standpoint was Ch. Sandy Hills Solar of Mylislee (bred by Phyllis Gillinger), sire of 18 champions. Another was Ch. Penthouse Premonition, a tri-color, who produced 11 champions.

"Nat," as Miss Maas was known, was a very dedicated person. She was also the Attorney for the American Spaniel Club for several years and is missed greatly.

The Hall-Way Kennels' foundation bitch was Hall-Way Panda-Monium, and they feel all of their later champions can trace back to her bloodlines. Their best known champion was Ch. Hall-Way Hoot Mon who sired 43 champions, including Ch. Scioto Bluff's Sinbad, the greatest producer of all time. Hoot Mon came from the mating of Ch. Hall-Way Honey Hue and Ch. Merlady Timmy. This decision to breed the solid to parti-color was made by Jim Hall, and while a complete outcross, turned out to be most fortunate.

Tad and Barbara Duncan of Flintcrest Kennels became interested in Cockers in the early 1960s. Their first Cocker was a birthday present for Barbara and luck was with them, as he became Am. and Can. Ch. Flintcrest Sin-Fan Smudge. Shortly after that, they met Beth and Jim Hall of Hall-Way fame, from whom they received a great deal of encouragement and help.

They then acquired a bitch named "Spook" through a breeding agreement. She was a black and white daughter of Ch. Rexpointe Frostee Dutchman and Ch. Hall-Way Hallelu. She proved a real credit to her owners by producing 11 champions. Her official name was Am. and Can. Ch. Hallway Fancy Free and she was bred by the Halls.

The Duncans' Ch. Fancy Free Carmen, bred by Mr. and Mrs. Keith Oswald, produced 10 champions. To date the Duncans have bred 17 champions.

The Jo-Be-Glen Kennels of Bea Muller contributed a great deal in building the quality and beauty of the buffs of today. She was the breeder of the two great producers, Ch. Artru Johnny Be Good, 52 champions, and Ch. Jo-Be-Glen Bronze Falcon, 43 champions.

Ch. Main-Dale's Mr. Success (whelped 1959), sire of 46 champions, most famous of the many outstanding show dogs bred by Dr. Carl Oldham.

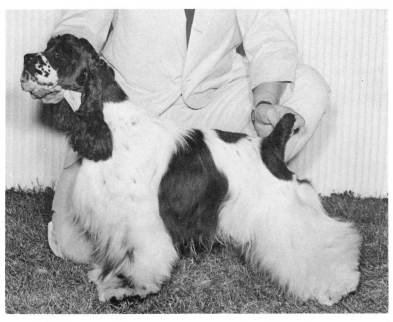

Ch. Hall-Way Hoot Mon, sire of 43 champions including the top Cocker sire of all time – Ch. Scioto Bluff's Sinbad. Bred and owned by Jim Hall.

Mrs. Byron Covey of Camby Cockers has bred 32 champions. Her greatest, Contribution, bred 26 and had a fine specials career. He was Best in Show at the National Specialty in 1967. Their most influential bitch was Ch. Camby's Susan. She was a top winner and produced 8 champions.

The Harlanhaven Kennels was started early in the fifties by Harlan Hoel, and later, Tom Stimfig joined him. While their original idea was to breed just buffs, they have managed to breed champions of all varieties.

Some 53 champions have carried the Harlanhaven prefix. Their most influential sire and winner is Ch. Harlanhaven Handsome, sire of 22 champions. Ch. Harlanhaven Hesitation and Ch. Harlanhaven Hope were their top producing dams with 4 champions each.

Mrs. Harry Reno has been consistently breeding show Cockers for many years. She has finished 20 champions—owner shown. Her Ch. Abbie's Mister Shadow Boy had a great show record and is producing well for her.

The Liz-Bar Kennels of Mr. and Mrs. Norman Barnes were very fortunate in having Charles Milwain and Henry Burson to help them on their way. By leasing a bitch from Larry Smith of Heyday Kennels, even though 4 years of age, she was finished by Charles Milwain and then bred to Hickory Hill High Catch, giving them their first champion, Liz-Bar Lucky Strike.

While blacks are their favorites, they have bred buffs and partis. They have finished 31 champions, the majority blacks. Fourteen still reside with them. Their present sensation, out with Don Johnston, is Ch. Liz-Bar Magic of Music. He is building a terrific record of Group wins, Bests of Breed, Bests in Show, and twice has been Best Black at the National Specialty.

Their top producer is Ch. Liz-Bar's Magician, sire of 12 champions.

The serious breeding of Dr. Owen Young of Kekko Kennels did not begin until 1967, although he had owned a couple of quality bitches before that time. His interest in showing began when he acquired a bitch named Junkin Chochosan. With the help of a couple of handlers, she soon became an American, Mexican and Canadian Champion.

She is presently the dam of 3 International Champions: Kekko's Kuroi Shinjusan, Kekko's Haru No-Hana and Kekko's Komadori. She is also the mother of several bitches in Mexico, also champions, and of three champion sons there.

108

Ch. Camby's Contribution, winner of the 1967 ASC National Specialty and the sire of 26 champions, greatest of the 32 champions bred by Mrs. Byron Covey, Camby Cockers.

Ch. Sandy Hills Solar of Mylislee (red/white, whelped 1970), sire of 18 champions. Bred by Phyllis Gillinger and owned by the late Natalie Maas.

In 1968, Ch. Hi-Jack's Holy Smoke was purchased and soon became America's first International Cocker Spaniel Champion, having acquired American, Mexican and Canadian titles. His daughter became the first International Champion bitch.

Two others, purchased as puppies have become International Champions: LaMar's Zoge Geisha and Kekko's Daikoku of Willowood. The latter, in addition to American, Mexican, and Canadian, obtained a Venezuelan title. There are five International Champions that reside at Kekko Kennels, and two others are on the way.

Dr. Young, a licensed psychologist, resides in Malibu on a hillside overlooking the sea. His involvement in the international scene has provided interest throughout the world. He has served as Chairman of the Relationship with Foreign Kennel Clubs Committee for the American Spaniel Club. This Committee's purpose is to bring information to the foreign kennel clubs and standardize the breed throughout the world.

Mary Joan and Cecil Replogle have been breeding for many years in Ohio. Ch. Merryhaven Strutaway was their most influential dog and, in addition, sired many top producers for their kennels. He stands as sire of 28 champions and the influence of Strutaway lives on through his direct tail line descendents of top producers.

Ch. Shoestring Shootin' Match, owned by Dr. Sarah E. Forbes is the sire of 20 champions.

Lucie and Bob Lake's Lurola Farm had its beginning as a serious show hobby in the middle fifties. Their first great show dog was Ch. Lurola's Leading Issue, who finished his championship in 1960. He had a great show career finishing top in the nation that year.

Their Lurola's Leilanni produced 9 champions from two sires. Six were by Ch. Lurola's Lookout, who produced 16 champions.

Ch. Lurola Royal Lancer has produced 40 champions to date and is still producing.

The Valli Lo Kennels of Mrs. John Brojanac, a top breeder during the early sixties, has produced 28 champions and her influence continues today in current blacks and black and tans. Her top producer was Ch. Valli Lo Flash Away, sire of 31 champions. Her top producing bitch was Ch. Valli Lo Vixen. She was influential in the breeding program of Ch. Baliwick Bebop, dam of 6 champions. Valli Lo is behind many of today's top winning and producing blacks and black and tans.

110

Ch. Merryhaven Strutaway, whelped 1957, sire of 28 champions. Owned by Cecil and Mary Joan Replogle.

Ch. Abbi's Mister Shadow Boy, buff whelped 1967, an outstanding show winner and one of 20 champions bred by Mrs. Harry Reno.

111

Ch. Hi-Boots Such Brass, one of the Top Ten Sporting Group winners in the mid-60s, and a great producer. Bred and owned by Dr. Alvin Grossman and his late wife, Marjorie.

Ch. Sanstar's Pied Piper, bred and owned by Irene L. Peacock, has produced 14 champions in the States and Canada.

oh Dell's Sashay, bred and
ned by Louis (Bud) and Ida
nsher, dam of 9 champions.

Ch. Shiloh Dell's Napoleon Solo,
bred by the Hamshers and owned
by Flo-Bob Kennels, sired 14
champions.

Shiloh Dell's Salute, whelped
9, sire of 30 champions. Bred
the Hamshers and owned by
Jason Abrams.

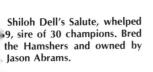

113

Dr. Alvin Grossman and the late Marjorie Grossman were the breeders of Ch. Hi-Boots Such Brass, a top sire and a great producer. Their contribution to the fancy came through their many articles and just recently, a book containing interesting information on breeding. Their top bitch was Hi-Boots Such Sass, which produced 4 champions.

Ch. BeGay Tan Man was bred and owned by Gay and the late Bill Ernst. He had a great show record and produced 28 champions. He was a top producer in 1969 and 1970.

Bill Ernst, breeder of BeGay Cockers, was a great handler and his loss to the fancy through his death from cancer in 1977, at the age of only 36, is deeply felt. He did a lot to stimulate interest in the chocolate color through his rare color program.

Ch. Baliwick Baghdad was bred by Melvin Colbert and owned and named by Norman Austin, who later sold him to Dr. William Fritz. Baghdad was sire of 32 champions and was a top producer in '65 and '67.

The Champagne Cocker Kennels of Joe and Dorothy Angerame started with the purchase of a silver buff puppy bitch in 1953 from the Shirwill-Joy-Pat Kennels of Shirley Currier and Evelyn Weiss. She was their foundation bitch and many of her very good qualities have been passed on to the many champions they have raised and finished.

Her first litter was by Walter Tuddenham's Ch. Lord Nelson of the Knoll. Ch. Champagne Black Knight, from this mating, went through to his championship in fast order. His litter sister, Champagne's Black Chiffon, proved an excellent producer and is behind many of their top winners.

Their champions are too numerous to list. Their Ch. Champagne's Dream Maker sired 12 champions and had a great specials career. Their Ch. Champagne's Dynamic is now being shown in specials with great success.

Ida and Louis (Bud) Hamsher acquired their first Cocker in 1953. He was not a show dog but a great obedience dog, earning a Utility degree. After contact with some beautiful show dogs, they acquired a bitch of good quality and bred her to Ch. Willowood Wampum. This produced their first litter which whelped in 1954.

The bug had bitten and from then on they, with the help of Dr. Oldham of Main-Dale fame, went forward with their breeding. One of their greatest producers was Ch. Shiloh Dell September Song, dam of 6

Ch. Lurola's Royal Lancer, black/tan whelped 1969, already the sire of 40 champions. Bred and owned by Bob and Luci Lake.

Ch. Champagne's Dynamic, owned by Joe and Dorothy Angerame, is being shown in Specials with great success. Here pictured winning BOB at the New England Specialty under judge Richard Thomas.

champions. Another great one was Ch. Shiloh Dell Sadie, who produced 8 champions.

Ch. Shiloh Dell's Napoleon Solo, who was sold to the Flo-Bob Kennels, sired 14 champions. Ch. Shiloh Dell's Salute, who was sold to Dr. Jason Abrams, sired 30 champions.

The Hamshers have bred 40 champions.

The Phi-Tau Kennels of Charles Cobb and John Gymer has been in existence for many years. Their greatest was Ch. Phi-Tau Prophet who sired 14 champions, including a Best in Show winner.

Winnie Vick's Bobwin Kennels has bred 15 champions since 1966. Her top winner was Ch. Bobwin's Boy Eagle, who sired 15 champions and had a fine specials career. Her top producing dam was Ch. Bobwin's Thumbalina, the dam of 6 champions.

Ch. Mijo's Martini, bred by Patricia Fender and owned by Hansi Rowland and Mildred Seger, is a buff sire of 10 champions.

Mrs. Helen Rice of the Corwin Kennels was the breeder of 20 champions. Her top producing sire was Ch. Corwin's Chances Are. Her most influential dam was Ch. Nor-Mar's Nice N' Neat, who founded a dynasty of top producing bitches through her daughters, Diamond Lil, Calico and My Cheri.

Another kennel that has been active continuously since 1951 is the Milru Kennels, owned by Ruth Muller and her late husband, Milt, of Long Island. They were active in both conformation and obedience through the past 25 years. Their foundation bitch, Milru's Licorice Honey, also had a U.D.T. in obedience. Her bloodlines were Ch. Jay's Extra Honey and Ch. Biggs' Cover Charge. The many champions they have produced go back to this foundation bitch, Extra Honey.

Ch. Alorah's Artful Dodger, owned by Alice and Debbie Schnabel, has had an outstanding career in the show ring and is now proving himself as a producer. He was the Number One Buff in 1976. The Schnabels have produced 7 champions and have many more nearly finished.

Ted and Lillian Klaiss bred their first litter in 1964 and since that time their success has been remarkable. From 14 litters have come 31 champions. Their greatest was Ch. Sagamore Toccoa. Sold as a

116

Ch. Windy Hill's Tis Demi Tasse, whose champion progeny includes Demon and the 1977 Futurity winner, Makes Its Point. Owned by Mrs. Edna T. Anselmi. Pictured being handled to win by the late Bill Ernst.

Ch. BeGay Tan Man was bred and owned by Gay and the late Bill Ernst. Bill is pictured handling Tan Man to BOV at the 1970 American Spaniel Club national Specialty under breeder-judge Dr. Gilbert Taylor.

Ch. Sagamore Happy Talk, dam of 8 champions including Ch. Sagamore Toccoa – the top winning Cocker of all time. Bred and owned by Ted and Lillian Klaiss.

Two fine representatives of Mrs. Edna T. Anselmi's Windy Hill Cockers. Left, the kennel's most influential stud has been Ch. Windy Hill's Tis Demi's Demon, sire of 17 champions. Right, its top winner has been Ch. Windy Hill's Eagle Scout.

Top producing dam of the Windy Hill Cockers is Ch. Windy Hill's Tis Tam Tam, CD, dam of 6 champions. Bred and owned by Mrs. Edna T. Anselmi.

Windy Hill's Makes Its Point, 1977 Futurity winner. Owned by Edna Anselmi.

119

youngster to Peggy Westphal and handled to her great record by Ted Young, Toccoa became the Top Winning Cocker Spaniel of all time. In 1972 she was the Top Winning Dog—All Breeds—in America, certainly a remarkable record.

The Klaiss' Ch. Sagamore Happy Talk produced 8 champions, including Toccoa. Ch. Sagamore Medallian produced 5 champions and their Colleen and Sprite had excellent show records.

Mrs. Edna T. Anselmi, of Windy Hill Cockers, has been a top breeder during the past few years. Her most influential stud has been Ch. Windy Hill's Tis Demi's Demon, sire of 17 champions. Her top producing dam is Ch. Windy Hills Tis Tam Tam, C.D., dam of 6 champions. Her top winner in the ring is Ch. Windy Hill Eagle Scout. Her Ch. Windy Hill Tis Velvet produced 4 champions.

Mrs. Anselmi believes that the more pups are handled in their early stage, the better they will be at maturity. She also feels that the visual study of puppies during their growing period is far better than studying pedigrees.

Lanebrook's Dash O'Flash, a black bitch bred and owned by Captain and Mrs. Stanley Chapman, produced 11 champions from three sires. Six were by Ch. Valli Lo's Viceroy.

Ch. Laurim's Command Performance, owned by Laurabeth and Dr. James R. Duncan, was sire of 15 champions. Their top winning bitch was Ch. Laurim's Star Performer. His top producing bitch was Ch. Fi Fo's Lovely Laurim.

Marion and Nancy Valasco have been dedicated Cocker enthusiasts for a number of years and, through trials and tribulations, they have finished 7 homebred champions. With their determination, they should finish many more.

Irene L. Peacock's Ch. Sanstar's Pied Piper has produced 14 champions in the States and 3 in Canada. His daughter, Ch. Sanstar's Joy Maker, was a top winning ASCOB bitch in 1974 and now is proving herself as a producer.

It is usually the males that set the fantastic records in the show ring, but over the last year (1977) three girls have really shown up a storm.

The black bitch, Ch. Tabaka's Tidbit O'Wynden, CDX., with her beautiful conformation and her smooth movement, has set quite a

Ch. Sanstar's Joy Maker, a top winning ASCOB bitch in 1974. Owned by Irene L. Peacock.

Ch. Alorah's Artful Dodger, the number 1 buff Cocker in the nation in 1976. Owned by Alice and Debbie Schnabel.

121

Ch. Glen Hollow Standout, bred and owned by Paul and Diane Lizotte. Glen Hollow Kennels has finished 15 champions.

Ch. Butch's King Coal, Best Black in Sweepstakes at the ASC National Specialty, July 1977. Bred and owned by Mr. and Mrs. Walter Thompson.

h. See Mar Nan Topy's Al, black, ed and owned by Marion and ancy Valasco. Al is the kennel's ghth champion.

h. Merlady's Mascot, foundation g of Marion and Nancy Valasco's See Mar Nan Kennels, Reg.

h. Ward's Martinet finishing to ampionship in 1976. The kennels of Mr. and Mrs. John S. Ward ve featured Cockers that have arred in conformation and Obedence. (Mr. Ward is author of the apter on Obedience in this ok.)

123

Ch. Russ' Winter Beauty, scintillating buff whelped 1974, is one of the top winning Cockers on the current scene, with a particularly strong record of Specialty wins. Bred and owned by Larry and Norma Russ. Pictured in her win of the 1977 CSC of Memphis Specialty under the author, with Mary Ellen Slobaski handling.

Ch. Frandee's Celebration, at this writing the top winning Parti-color on the West Coast. Owned by Frank and Dee Dee Wood.

record in show and obedience rings. She is owned by Ruth Tabaka and Wynn Bloch.

Tidbit, handled to earlier success by Jim Hall in the West, is at this writing being handled to spectacular winning in the East by Ted Young. Her Bests in Show there include win of the National Specialty in January 1977.

The lovely golden buff bitch, Ch. Russ' Winter Beauty, has been winning Varieties and Group placements over some of the top specials. She was Best of Variety at Westminster and many other top shows. She is owned by Larry and Norma Russ.

And now, another girl from the West Coast, Ch. Frandee's Celebration, is busy showing the boys that the girls can win too. She is presently top winning parti-color in the West, and is winning many Varieties and Groups. She is owned by Frank and Dee Dee Wood.

Show records and producing records of Cocker Spaniels throughout the country have been phenomenal during the past decade. I have endeavored to mention as many as possible, but limitations were inevitable. My sincere apologies for any that have been overlooked.

TOP PRODUCERS

The Foremost Sires

On the facing page:

The top Cocker sire of all time—Ch. Scioto Bluff's Sinbad, sire of 118 champions. Bred and owned by Charles D. and Veda L. Winders. Pictured in his win of Best in Show at the 1962 American Spaniel Club National Specialty under judge Mrs. H. Terrell Van Ingen (of Pinefair Kennels fame), with Ron Fabis handling.

```
                    Merlady Happy Lad
          Ch. Merlady Timmy
                    Cricket's Bubble Dancer
    Ch. Hall-Way Hoot Mon
                         Ch. Gravel Hill Gold Opportunity
          Ch. Hall-Way Honey Hue
                         Ch. Hall-Way Haughty
CH. SCIOTO BLUFF'S SINBAD – red and white (whelped 1959)
                              Ch. Mar-Hawk's Gift to Glenshaw
              Ch. Baliwick Brandy
                         Ch. Rebel Ridge Fancyfree
    Ch. Scioto Bluff's Judy
                    Creekwood Chessman
          Creekwood Miss Showoff
                         Ch. Honey Creek Havana
```

The top non-titled sire in Cocker history – Orient's It's A Pleasure, sire of 101 champions. Owned by Al and Dorothy Orient.

Ch. Poling's Smoky Shadow
　　Ch. Poling's Imurguy
　　Poling's Dottie
Ch. Poling's Gay Blade
　　Ch. Mar-Hawk's O'Riley
　　Ch. Poling's So Lovely
　　Poling's Autumn Maid
ORIENT'S IT'S A PLEASURE — red and white (whelped 1960)
　　Ch. Dun-Mar's Dapper Dan
　　Ch. Dau-Han's Dan Morgan
　　Ch. Dau-Han's Holiday Flirt
Ch. Orient's Truly Yours
　　Ch. Hall-Way Hooligan
　　Norbill's Novelty
　　Norbill's Painted Daisy

The top living Cocker sire – Ch. Dreamridge Dominoe (right), to date the sire of 81 champions. With him is Ch. Dreamridge Dinner Date, dam of 9 champions including Dominoe. Both owned by Tom O'Neal.

```
                                    Ch. Merlady Timmy
                          Ch. Hall-Way Hoot Mon
                                    Ch. Hall-Way Honey Hue
               Ch. Scioto Bluff's Sinbad
                                    Ch. Baliwick Brandy
                          Ch. Scioto Bluff's Judy
                                    Creekwood Miss Showoff
CH. DREAMRIDGE DOMINOE – black and white (whelped 1968)
                                    Ch. Baliwick Baghdad
                          Ch. Clarkdale Calcutta
                                    Ch. Clarkdale Chickadee
               Ch. Dreamridge Dinner Date
                                    Ch. Scioto Bluff's Sinbad
                          Pounette Perrette
                                    Ch. Pounette Fancy Dancer
```

Ch. Stockdale Town Talk, whelped in 1939. In his time the foremost sire of the breed, and still the No. 1 black producer with 80 champions. An outstanding showman, his wins included the Sporting Group at Westminster 1945. Bred by Mrs. Stephanie T. Adams, he was owned and guided to his greatness by C. B. Van Meter, pictured with him here.

```
                                    Ch. Torohill Trader
                        Noble Sir
                                    My Own Blacklocks
            Ch. Argyll's Archer
                                    Sandy of Irolita
                        Sand Spring Smile Awhile
                                    Ch. Sand Spring Smiling Through
CH. STOCKDALE TOWN TALK – black (whelped 1939)
                                    Ch. Sand Spring Stormalong
                        Ch. Stockdale Startler
                                    Stockdale Miss Manning
            Audacious Lady
                                    Rowcliffe Amber Rust
                        Black Winnie
                                    Mariquita Cinders
```

Ch. Clarkdale Capital Stock, sire of 76 champions. Capital Stock was one of the Top Ten of the Sporting Group in America from 1958 through 1960. Bred and owned by Mr. and Mrs. Leslie Clark.

Ch. Myroy Night Rocket
Ch. Elderwood Bangaway
Ch. Elder's So Lovely
Ch. DeKarlo's Dashaway
Ch. Lancaster Great Day
Ch. DeKarlos Miss Dorothy
Lancaster Shades of Nowanda
CH. CLARKDALE CAPITAL STOCK — black (whelped 1957)
Ch. Myroy Night Rocket
Ch. Elderwood Bangaway
Ch. Elder's So Lovely
Ch. Clarkdale Closing Quotation
Van Valzah's King of Hearts
Ch. Clarkdale Copper Valentine
Van Valzah's Viking Girl

131

Ch. Crackerbox Certainly, sire of 72 champions. Bred and owned by Mr. and Mrs. Robert Graham, Jr.

```
                              Ch. Myroy Night Rocket
                    Ch. Elderwood Bangaway
                              Ch. Elder's So Lovely
          Ch. Baliwick Banter
                              Ch. Lancaster Great Day
                    Ch. Genesee Great Daisy
                              Ch. Genesee Joyful
CH. CRACKERBOX CERTAINLY – black and tan (whelped 1956)
                              Ch. Lancaster Landmark
                    Ch. St. Andrea's Medicine Man
                              Jubilo Madcap
          Ch. Crackerbox Collar and Cuffs
                              Ch. Stockdale Town Talk
                    Ch. Lancaster Nowanda's Pride
                              Ch. Nonquitt Nowanda
```

Ch. Artru Sandpiper, sire of 66 champions including the all-time top winning Cocker, Ch. Sagamore Toccoa. Bred by Corinne Karcher and owned and shown by Art and Ruth Benhoff.

```
                                              Ch. Artru Crackerjack
                              Ch. Artru Hot Rod
                                              Pett's Ragtime Rhythm, C.D.
              Ch. Artru Johnny Be Good
                                              Ch. Jo-Be-Glen's Gold Cross
                              Jo-Be-Glen's Honeycomb
                                              Jo-Be-Glen's Sunbeam
CH. ARTRU SANDPIPER – buff (whelped 1965)
                                              Ch. Artru Hot Rod
                              Ch. Charma's Mr. O'Harrigan
                                              Ch. Bridey Murphy II
              Ch. Bar-C-Kar's Peau Rouge
                                              Ch. Artru Sir Upnor
                              Artru Bar-C-Kar
                                              Carolina's Sweet 'N Lovely
```

Am. & Can. Ch. Maddie's Vagabond's Return, sire of 60 champions. An outstanding winner of many Bests in Show and Groups in his time. Bred and owned by Madeline E. Pequet, he was handled by Parley Larabee.

Ch. Ossie's Smooth Sailing

Ch. Arno's Statesman

Ossie's Apple Blossom

Poling's Royal Splendor

Poling's Black Hurricane

Poling's Misty Girl

Poling's Canola

INT. CH. MADDIE'S VAGABOND'S RETURN – buff (whelped 1949)

Ch. Easdale's Excellency

Ch. Lee'Eb's Royal Cavalier

Lee-Eb's Ginger Snap

Lee-Eb's Sweetie Pie

Ch. Sunny Jim O'Flint

Lee-Eb's Golden Jewel

Lee-Eb's Red Sunglow II

Ch. Hob-Nob-Hill's Tribute, sire of 54 champions. Tribute's outstanding show career included wins of an all-breed Best in Show, 10 Groups and 10 Bests in Specialty. Bred by Kay and Larry Hardy and owned by Dr. and Mrs. Clarence A. Smith. (Pictured winning BOB at Cocker Spaniel Club of New Jersey 1966 Specialty under judge Richard Thomas; Charlotte Stacy handling.)

Ch. Benwood Rockaway

Ch. Merryhaven Strutaway

Merryhaven Merrianne

Ch. Hob Nob Hill's Hob Nobber

Ch. Hearthcote Here's Jeffrey

Ch. Hob Nob Hill's Yumberry

Ch. Hob Nob Hill Enchanting

CH. HOB-NOB-HILL'S TRIBUTE – black (whelped 1964)

Ch. Gravel Hill Gold Opportunity

Ch. Kay's Hob Nob Hill Hifalutin'

Hardy's Waggely Anne

Hob Nob Hill's Look Me Over

Ch. Shady Glenn Mr. Mixer Upper

Pett's Imp of White Satin

Pett's Divine

Ch. Artru Johnny Be Good, sire of 52 champions. A consistent winner of the late '60s. Bred by Bernice and John Muller and owned by Art and Ruth Benhoff.

                                     Ch. Ca-Da's Allegrante of Woodbine
                      Ch. Artru Crackerjack
                                    Harness Creek Miss Artru
           Ch. Artru Hot Rod
                                 Ch. Glo's Gay Echo
                         Pett's Ragtime Rhythm, C.D.
                                 Ragtime Merry Mischief
CH. ARTRU JOHNNY-BE-GOOD – silver buff (whelped 1961)
                               Ch. Eufaula's Dividend
                     Ch. Jo-Be-Glen's Gold Cross
                               Jo-Be-Glen's Saucy Suzy
         Jo-Be-Glen's Honeycomb
                               Big Top's First Performer
                 Jo-Be-Glen's Sunbeam
                               Jo-Be-Glen's Claudia

Ch. Rinky Dink's Sir Lancelot, already the sire of 48 champions. Bred and owned by Jean and Bill Peterson. Pictured scoring BOV at 1975 Maryland Specialty under judge Edward Bracy. Handled by Charlotte Stacy.

Baliwick Bangaway
Am. Can. Ch. Lurola's Lookout
Lurola's Lucky Lady
Am. Can. Ch. Har-Dee's High Spirit
Ch. Har-Dee's Headlites
Ch. Har-Dee's Hi-Style
Har-Dee's Kandee Kisses
CH. RINKY DINK'S SIR LANCELOT – black and tan (whelped 1972)
Ch. Hopewood's Headstrong
Robin Knoll's Suppose
Ch. Robin Knoll's Amber
Ch. Rinky Dink's Robin
Ch. Har-Dee's Hell Bender II
Dawn's Harem Queen
Dawn's Honey Babe

137

Ch. Artru Action sired 48 champions.

<pre>
                        Ch. Artru Hot Rod
                 Ch. Artru Johnny Be Good
                        Jo-Be-Glen's Honeycomb
           Ch. Artru Sandpiper
                        Ch. Charma's Mr. O'Harrigan
                 Ch. Bar-C-Kar's Peau Rouge
                        Artru Bar-C-Kar
CH. ARTRU ACTION — buff (whelped 1968)
                        Ch. Hollyrock Helmsman
                 Ch. Hollyrock Harvester
                        Gardenhouse Hermia
           Van-Dor Fancy Trianne
                        Ch. Vadelmar's Gay Blade
                 Mione Red Amber
                        Mione How Fancy
</pre>

The Foremost Dams

*Ch. Seenar's Seductress is the top producing dam
in Cocker history — dam of 15 champions. Bred
and owned by Ramona and Carl Cantrell.*

<pre>
                        Ch. Hickory Hill High Jack
                 Ch. Hickory Hill High Bracket
                        Hickory Hill Holly
           Ch. Ram-Bow's Rambler, C.D.X.
                        Luck of Heather's Belvedere
                 Bejak's Lucky Heather, C.D.X.
                        Attention Sparkette
CH. SEENAR'S SEDUCTRESS — black (whelped 1965)
                        Ch. Crackerbox Certainly
                 Ch. Palmwood Promenader
                        Ch. Palmwood Ace High Pattern
           Palmwood Pantomine
                        Ch. Hickory Hill High Catch
                 Ch. Palmwood Pamela
                        Ch. Sugarbrook Enchanting
</pre>

138

Int. Ch. Honey Creek Vivacious produced 14 champions, She stands as the top producing Parti dam.

<pre>
                            Ch. Bobb's Master Showman
                    Ch. Bobb's Showmaster
                            Bobb's Dream Lady
            Int. Ch. Sogo Showoff
                            Ch. Hadley's Trumpeter
                    Sogo Suzette
                            Ch. Blackstone Barette
INT. CH. HONEY CREEK VIVACIOUS – red and white (whelped 1947)
                            Ch. Easdale's Winsome Laddie
                    Ch. Young's Laddie Boy
                            Mistwood Evening Song
            Ch. Honey Creek Cricket
                            Ch. Bobb's Showmaster
                    Ch. Honey Creek Sue
                            Honey Creek Flicka
</pre>

Artru Delightful II produced 14 champions – the top producing ASCOB dam in Cocker history.

<pre>
                            Ch. Artru Johnny Be Good
                    Ch. Artru Sandpiper
                            Ch. Bar-C-Bar's Peau Rouge
ARTRU DELIGHTFUL II – buff (whelped 1969)
                            Ch. Ca-Da's Plum Brandy
                    Request Plum Delightful
                            Pen Del Burgundy Quest
</pre>

Ch. Hickory Hill High Night produced 11 champions.

<pre>
                            Ch. Gravel Hill Hallmark
                    Ch. Sugarbrook Counterpoint
                            The Belle of Littlebrook
            Ch. Taylor's Dark Night
                            Penrock's Pied Piper
                    Sugarbrook Fancy
                            Little Brook Gypsy Princess
CH. HICKORY HILL HIGH NIGHT – black (whelped 1964)
                            Ch. Argyll's Archer
                    Ch. Stockdale Town Talk
                            Audacious Lady
            Ch. Hickory Hill High Barbaree
                            Dungarvan D. Day
                    Ch. Hickory Hill High Bid
                            Hickory Hill High Heels
</pre>

Lanebrook's Dash O'Flash, dam of
11 champions. Owned by Captain
and Mrs. Stanley Chapman.

Ch. Elderwood Bangaway
Ch. DeKarlos Dashaway
Ch. DeKarlos Miss Dorothy
Ch. Valli-Lo's Flashaway
Dun-Mar's Diplomat
Chuck O'Luck's Cassandra
Coull's Carla
LANEBROOK DASH O'FLASH – black (whelped 1964)
Ch. DeKarlo's Dashaway
Ch. Clarkdale Capital Stock
Ch. Clarkdale Closing Quotation
Meri Glad's Miniature
Ch. Crackerbox Certainly
Ch. Meriglad's Magnificence
Ch. Dorey's Bonus Baby

Am. & Can. Ch. Hall-Way Fancy Free, dam of 11 champions. Bred by Mr. and Mrs. Jim Hall and owned by Ted and Barbara Duncan of Flintcrest Kennels.

Ch. Glenshaw's Captain Kidd
Ch. Rexpointe Captain Holiday
Hall-Way Holiday
Ch. Rexpointe Frostee Dutchman
Ch. Maribeau's Mid-Summer Madness
Ch. Maribeau's My Lil' Dutch Treat
Maribeau's My Treat
AM. AND CAN. CH. HALL-WAY FANCY FREE – black and white (whelped 1961)
Silverylane Snowball
Norbill's High and Mighty
Norbill's Fancy Affair
Ch. Hall-Way Hallelu
Ch. Gravel Hill Gold Opportunity
Ch. Hall-Way Hedy
Ch. Hall-Way Haughty

141

Ch. Bar-C-Kar's Peau Rouge produced 11 champions.

Ch. Artru Crackerjack
Ch. Artru Hot Rod
Pett's Ragtime Rhythm
Am. and Can. Ch. Charma's Mr. O'Harrigan
Ca-Da's Gadabout
Ch. Bridey Murphy II
Ca-Da's Maureen
CH. BAR-C-KAR'S PEAU ROUGE – red and white (whelped 1961)
Ch. Artru Hot Rod
Ch. Artru Sir Upnor
Ch. Silver Dust of Upnor
Artru Bar-C-Kar
Ch. Carolina Yankee Doodle Dandy
Carolina's Sweet N' Lovely
Carolina Moon Mist

Ch. Fi-Fo's Fiesta produced 10 champions.

Ch. Scioto Bluff's Sinbad
Ch. Baliwick Baghdad
Clarkdale Country Cathy
CH. FI-FO'S FIESTA – tricolored (whelped 1947)
Ch. Scioto Bluff's Sinbad
Ch. Fi-Fo's Madam Spook
Fi-Fo's Untouchable

Ch. Essenar Evening Song produced 10 champions.

Ch. Mijo's Martini
Ch. Wistful Wears My Heart
Ch. Mijo's Miss B Haven
CH. ESSANAR EVENING SONG – black (whelped 1967)
Ch. Har-Dee's Hell Bender 11
Ch. Har- Dee's Heart-Beat
Ch. Har-Dee's Fancy Doll

142

Ch. Honey Creek Cricket produced 10 champions.

Ch. Scioto Request
Ch. Easdale's Winsome Laddie
Scioto Pierrette
Ch. Young's Laddie Boy
Scioto Sand Idol
Mistwood Evening Song
Scioto Zara
CH. HONEY CREEK CRICKET – red and white (whelped 1945)
Ch. Bobb's Master Showman
Ch. Bobb's Showmaster
Bobb's Dream Lady
Ch. Honey Creek Sue
Essendale Promotion
Honey Creek Flicka
Honey Creek Freckles

Ch. Frandee's Susan is dam of 10 champions.

Ch. Camby's Contribution
Sonata's Holiday Caper
Ch. Sonata's Justin Hope
CH. FRANDEE'S SUSAN – black and white (whelped 1969)
Ch. Gin-Di's Tri By Jiminy
Am. & Mex. Ch. Corwin's Diamond Lil
Ch. Normar's Nice 'N' Neat

Ch. Hickory Hill High Barbaree produced 10 champions.

Noble Sir
Ch. Argyll's Archer
Sand Spring Smile Awhile
Ch. Stockdale Town Talk
Ch. Stockdale Startler
Audacious Lady
Black Winnie
CH. HICKORY HILL HIGH BARBAREE – black (whelped 1947)
Ch. Gilfran's Getaway
Dungarvan D. Day
Dungarvan Judy
Ch. Hickory Hill High Bid
Ch. Covered Brook Bombardier
Hickory Hill High Heels
Heartsease Sharon

143

Ch. Misty Mornin' Motif was dam of 10 champions.

                              Ch. Gravel Hill Hallmark
                        Ch. Sugarbrook Counterpoint
                              The Belle of Little Brook
                  Ch. Hickory Hill High Catch
                                    Ch. Hickory Hill High Ho Silver
                        Hickory Hill Holly
                                    Ch. Hickory Hill High Bid
CH. MISTY MORNIN' MOTIF – black (whelped 1958)
                              Ch. Gravel Hill Hallmark
                        Ch. Sugarbrook Counterpoint
                              The Belle of Little Brook
                  Hickory Hill High Pitch
                                    Ch. Hickory Hill High Ho Silver
                        Hickory Hill Holly
                                    Ch. Hickory Hill High Bid

Ch. Nor-Mar's Nice and Neat was dam of 10 champions.

                              Ch. Maribeau's Mid-Summer Madness
                        Ch. Maribeau's Mid-Summer Eclipse
                              Wilhall Tranquility
                  Ch. Meriday's Tri-Sox
                                    Ch. Timberlane Yule Tide
                        Meriday's Mischief Miss
                                    Ch. Meriday's Merry Miss
CH. NOR-MAR'S NICE AND NEAT – black and white (whelped 1961)
                              Ch. Hall-Way Haughty Heir
                        Ven. Ch. Bar-Cliff's Best Bet For Nor-Mar
                              Ch. Sara's Snow Boots
                  Ch. Nor-Mar's Nettie
                                    Ch. Gail's Jiminy Cricket
                        Gail's Miss Topsy
                                    Gail's Tawny Patches

144

Pounette Perrette produced 10 champions.

Ch. Merlady Timmy
Ch. Hall-Way Hoot Mon
Ch. Hall-Way Honey Hue
Ch. Scioto Bluff's Sinbad
Ch. Baliwick Brandy
Ch. Scioto Bluff's Judy
Creekwood Miss Showoff
POUNETTE PERRETTE – red and white (whelped 1964)
Ch. Dun-Mar's Dapper Dan
Ch. Dau-Han's Dan Morgan
Ch. Dau-Han's Holiday Flirt
Ch. Pounette Fancy Dancer
Artru Tick Tock
Artru Pounette
Bellanca Bewitched

Ch. Fancy Free Carmen produced 10 champions.

Ch. Hall-Way Hoot Mon
Ch. Scioto Bluff's Sinbad
Ch. Scioto Bluff's Judy
Ch. Stonewalk Sharpshooter
Norbill's High & Mighty
Ch. Norbill's Heavenly
Ch. Norbill's Twinkling Star
CH. FANCY-FREE CARMEN – red and white (whelped 1964)
Ch. Dun-Mar's Dapper Dan
Ch. Grymesby Dan Slam
Ch. Grymesby Slipper Satin
Danzata Dotted Frock
Ch. Dun-Mar's Dapper Dan
Ch. Grymesby Fashion Frock
Ch. Grymesby Slipper Satin

145

Ch. Silver Maple Touch O'Tiger, a top current black, shown following his win of the Group at Cincinnati in May 1977. Owned by Silver Maple Kennels.

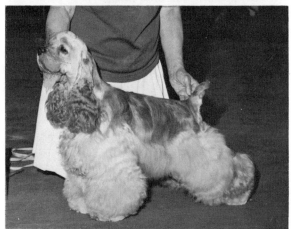

Ch. Artru Getaway, handsome buff, pictured scoring 3-point major on way to his 1974 championship.

Ch. Dreamridge Don Juan, a top current Parti, pictured following his win of the Group at Cornhusker Kennel Club, 1976. Owned by Tom O'Neal.

5

Cocker Spaniel Colors

THE COCKER FANCY is fortunate in that they are given an attractive variety of colors from which to choose. The color specifications for each of the varieties are carefully spelled out in the official breed standard (*see Chapter 8*).

Originally all the Cockers (including the English variety) were shown as one in the Sporting Group. When the Cocker popularity became such that they overwhelmed the entries and separation made sense for the operation of shows, the American Kennel Club assented to having the parti-colors shown as an entity in the Group. The English variety was designated a breed to itself. Then the ASCOBs and the black and tans were designated a variety for separate status. A move (around 1950) to have the black and tans designated a separate variety from the ASCOBs was not approved by the AKC.

The blacks have been a basic of the breed since Obo II. They are always beautiful and have been a favorite of many breeders and fanciers for years.

The ASCOB variety (any solid color other than black, to include black and tans) covers a multitude of colors. Buffs come in various shades from the very light color (often called silver) to the golden and reds. The browns and chocolates also come under this variety.

The tan markings of the black and tans must be definite and readily visible in the ring, and must be present in specific locations of the body noted in the standard.

147

Ch. Kaplar's Kopi-Kat, black and tan, scoring a strong Best of Breed at the Southern New Jersey CSC Specialty, 1975 under judge Mrs. A. Feinberg. Shown by breeder-owner Laura Henson.

Ch. Windridge Chocolate Comment taking his fourth major and finishing under Anne Rogers Clark.

148

The ASCOB variety also includes the brown and tans, a combination we may be seeing more of in the near future.

In the black and ASCOB varieties a small amount of white on the throat and chest is a penalty, but not a disqualification. White in any other location is a disqualification.

The parti-colors (which surprisingly antedate the blacks in Cocker history) can be any of the above colors with a contrasting background. The Standard calls for two or more definite colors appearing in clearly defined markings distributed over the body. More than 90% of primary color, or a secondary color limited solely to one location shall disqualify.

Roar.s are considered parti-colors and may be of any of the usual roaning patterns (mixtures of two or more colors in the coat). Tricolors are any of the above colors combined with tan markings.

Interest in the brown Cocker Spaniel makes for an interesting story and here we have it told by the lady most active in its development:

THE STORY OF THE "BROWNS"
by Arlene Swalwell, Windridge Kennels
The "Grandmother" of most of the brown
Cockers being shown today tells her story.

Many years ago, in fact in 1950, I bred a little black bitch named Chloe of Aldermyr to her red son Windridge Heads I Win (so named because of his extremely beautiful head).

I made that close breeding because I wanted to cinch that head beauty for my line. On January 3, 1951, she whelped her litter of three female puppies. One buff, one black, and one chocolate brown. The brown I named Windridge Brown Betty and kept her because of her unusual color.

On checking pedigrees, I found that the gene for brown had been in my stock for ten generations—but, it took that close breeding to bring it to the fore. The brown ancestor was the famous Sweet Georgia Brown.

From then on, it was a matter of finding by test breedings which of my buffs and blacks carried the brown gene.

There were only two buff females and one deep red that ever produced browns at that time. I had little to work with, but I felt that the color was so beautiful and the type was excellent for that day.

In 1955, the red bitch, Windridge Summer Star was bred to the black son of Ch. Carmor Rise and Shine and Windridge Brown Betty. His

149

name was Windridge Shoeshine Boy. This produced my first brown male, Windridge Collectors Item, who must be behind every winning brown today.

With so little to work with, it has been a long, hard pull to accomplish what I wished for. I had many beautiful buffs and blacks (37 champions, eleven of them both American and Canadian) and the brown color meant nothing to me unless the quality was tops. Fortunately in every litter where there were browns, blacks, and buffs, the browns were the outstanding puppies.

I have carried out the same line breeding with an occasional outcross that I practiced in my buffs and the results have been more than I had hoped for. The present day browns are gorgeous specimens and I am proud to say that every brown dog winning today carries my bloodlines.

Windridge Chocolate Rythm was the first brown female to be shown. She took two Best of Winners, but I did not try to finish her because I felt it much more important to use her for breeding.

Her first litter produced a brown male purchased at eight weeks by Elaine Poole. He became Windridge Chocolate Baron (Champion). I believe he is also a Mexican and French Champion and he now resides with Madame Rufer in France. He has been the foundation for the browns in France and a full color picture of him appeared on the cover of the French magazine *Chiens 2000*. His son Ch. Merribarks Mr. Brown is one of the top brown winners in the ring today.

Marline Moline waited many months for a chocolate male and when one was available, she purchased a puppy that became one of my first brown champions, Windridge Chocolate Dandy. His younger brother, Windridge Chocolate Chips, became the first brown champion here in my kennel, He is still with me although no longer used at stud. Dandy is the grand sire of Ch. Modernas Brown Derby, owned by Frances Greer.

Later, I showed for the first time as a puppy, the bitch Windridge Chocolate Puff. Norman Austin was at ringside that day. Puff went Reserve Winners and Norman could hardly wait to phone Frances Greer to tell her that he had found the perfect mate for her Ch. Modernas Brown Derby. Frances purchased her and I believe that it was after Puff was bred to Derby that the Birchwood Kennels acquired her; so she is the foundation for the Birchwood browns.

Bill Ernst's long line of browns with several winners started with Ch. Be Gays Harry Hershey, bred by Ruth Gilbertson, here in California and from Windridge stock. She now has a very handsome brown dog

150

Windridge Chocolate Rhythm, owned and handled by Arlene Swalwell.

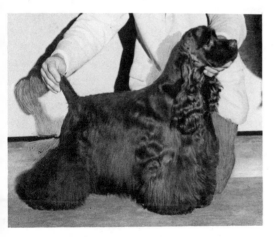

Ch. Windridge Chocolate Dandy. The first Windridge chocolate brown to complete his championship.

151

named Ch. Argyles Coco Caravelle, who has several Bests of Variety to his credit.

My latest chocolate, Ch. Windridge Chocolate Comment, finished with four majors.

Windridge Just a Doll out of Windridge Shining Star (a Carmor Rise and Shine daughter) and sired by Our Ridge Gay Cavalier, proved to be our first dependable producer of the chocolate color. She was the dam of Ch. Windridge Chocolate Dandy, Ch. Windridge Chocolate Chips, Windridge Chocolate Rythm and Windridge Chocolate Supreme.

Several outcrosses have been made in my brown line. The resulting offspring were black, buff, and red. The best were retained for breeding back to the browns or producers of browns. From these second generations have come some of the finest browns produced at Windridge.

Collection Item was a streamlined dog, well up on leg with what might now be called an old fashioned head. But, with careful breeding, we have produced browns with heads equal to and often surpassing many of the buffs and blacks in the ring today.

We found that if the outcross bitches (whether black, buff or red) had one brown parent they would definitely produce browns when bred to a brown or to a black or buff that carried the gene for brown. In other words, the gene for brown must be in both parents in order for them to produce browns. I call them chocolates because when seen beside a liver English Cocker, the Windridge browns are a much richer color than true liver and with shiny coats and profuse feathering.

Interestingly, the chocolate puppies have very blue eyes when they first open. They gradually turn to green and then slowly to a golden brown, which in most specimens deepens in color as the dog matures. Also, some of the brown puppies have very pink noses at birth, but we have never had one that did not deepen to a rich brown at maturity. In our more recent litters, we have eliminated the pink noses completely and the puppies are born with a rich brown leather.

Some of the young breeders of browns say never to breed brown to brown. That might be good advice in the beginning of your breeding program, but after almost thirty years of concentrating on this color, I can say that our most beautiful specimens are coming from brown to brown breeding.

Occasionally in a brown to brown breeding, we get a light nosed, amber-eyed buff. The coat color tends toward apricot. Some breeders discard these in their breeding program, but we have found them valuable as producers. When bred carefully, they produce dark-eyed and dark-leathered browns.

152

Am., Mex. and French Ch. Windridge Chocolate Baron. Sire of
Merribarks Mr. Brown. Now
owned by Mme. Reifer in France.

Ch. Merribarks Mr. Brown.
Owned by Elane Poole.

Ch. Modernas Brown Derby.
Owned by Frances Greer.

153

Ch. BeGay's Harry Hershey, whelped 1970, Bill Ernst's first brown champion. Bred by Ruth Gilbertson.

It is said that breeding two light-nosed, amber-eyed buffs will never produce browns. We have never made such a breeding, but we have produced a brown from a black to black breeding. The Windridge browns of excellent quality are now with responsible breeders in many states here in America and also in three countries in Europe. Therefore, the future looks very bright for this color. Almost every mail brings inquiries, and I cannot begin to supply the demand.

Caring for the coat on a brown is very little different from caring for the coat on another color Cocker, but they must be kept out of direct sunlight to keep the color dark and even.

A recent book on the Cocker Spaniel states that the coats on the browns are inclined to be wooly. This is not true in my Windridge strain. Perhaps the wooly coats come from poor diet. I use canned chicken entirely instead of beef, and I add to each feed pan every day one heaping teaspoonful of brewers yeast, four drops of vitamin E and a bottle cap full of peanut oil. If you do have a brown with a wool-like coat, plucking with a thumb and forefinger as you would with a terrier will probably help to correct it.

Because of my age and the impossibility of getting reliable kennel help at a price that I can afford, I will in the near future retire as a breeder of chocolates. However, I feel that this beautiful color will never again disappear from the show ring.

Ch. Ar-Gyle Coco Caravelle. Breeder-Owner Ruth Gilbertson.

Ch. Windridge Chocolate Classic, taking a 5 point major at Fresno Specialty.

Am. & Can. Ch. Magicours Monitor winning Best at Montreal. Monitor was Top Sporting Dog of Canada in 1966. Bred by Richard Thomas and owned by Norma and Anthony Donderwitz.

Mrs. Jean Hallett showing Shadyhill's Marcy (black) and Mrs. Dorothy Campbell showing Can. Ch. Camfield's Birthday Party, both owner-bred and handled.

6

The Cocker Spaniel in Canada

by Mrs. Norma Donderwitz

THE AMERICAN COCKERS in Canada have made great progress in quality and type in the last thirty years. From a type resembling the English Cocker with the longer body, longer foreface and sparse coat, the breeders have come up with the present day type of shorter bodies, better toplines, improved heads and expression. They also have good dispositions. In other words, here is a Cocker that can hold its own in competition anywhere.

It has not been an easy achievement, mainly because top stock was not available to the Canadian breeders. Few breeders were able to attend the shows in the United States where they could purchase good stock. They bought sight unseen and usually would end up "stuck." They paid an enormous price for inferior stock, something which a United States breeder did not want and would never see again. When the dog could not win or produce good progeny, the breeder was discouraged and his money had been spent.

However, several determined breeders hung on. The Try-Cob and Stockdale lines, later the Honey Creek and Silver Maple, to mention a few, found their way up here and slowly a better type and improved dispositions were developed.

157

Ch. Kobbytown's Cappie finishing to his championship. Bred and owned by Mr. and Mrs. Anthony Donderwitz.

From the Ottawa area, Can. Ch. Canbream's Toastmistress, bred and shown by Carol Parsons.

158

From the past, we see the names of Roy Bough of Bougholme Kennels, who did much to improve the blacks. With his handler, Walter Martin, this kennel dominated the shows for many years.

In the Ottawa area, we recall the nice blacks of Lorne Moore and the partis of Jack Farmer.

On the East Coast, we come up with the top winning black American and Canadian Champion Penhorn's Son of Prophet, who was owned by the MacNeils of Dartmouth, Nova Scotia. He was shown in the States by Clint Callahan.

The other top winning black boy was Ch. Alhambra Kingfish, shown in the U.S. by Norman Austin and in Canada by Walter Martin and Mr. Kylie.

Among the older names in the Toronto area we find the Merryway of Miss K. Balshaw, noted for her partis; the Bucksburn Kennels of Mrs. Munckton (blacks); Vaughnhaven (black and black and tans) and the Gayholme buffs of the Paul Daveys. The Daveys were among the first to organize the Cocker Spaniel Club of Central Ontario. Then, there was Mrs. Knox with her buffs from the Biggs lines.

A little later came the names of Marbrucken (black and partis); Namac; Wagaway; Sunny Hill; Carroll and, in Ottawa area, the La Paloma who exhibited all varieties.

The Blomidon Kennels played a big part in improving the partis in the Toronto area and their lines and kennel are still active today.

The Dennvabar partis and buffs were active for years.

Then we come to the Keljeager pretty buffs and black and tans, still active and winning and so capably handled by owner Jean Palmer.

No kinder lady to dogs has existed than Mrs. Kathryn Sandor of Toronto. She has given a home to many retired Cockers no longer wanted by their owners, and yet she, herself, has kept active in breeding and exhibiting many fine blacks and partis.

Later, we see the name of Valhar, the Orient line and the Bernandale partis and buffs.

In the Ottawa area again, we see the name of Nirvana, owned by Captain and Mrs. Willis, known for their partis, and their daughter with her pretty blacks and black and tans of the Morganne Kennel.

Most of these kennels are no longer with us, due to deaths of owners, sickness or transfer of locations, but all have left a big impact on the improvement of the Cocker.

Now, on the far East Coast, we see the present name of Shady Hill, owned by Jean Hallett, founded on the Kobbytown line. During the past fifteen years, Jean has come up with top blacks and black and tans.

159

Dorothy Campbell is breeding and showing nice partis from the Halifax area.

We see the four varieties, including chocolates, bred and handled by Denzil Thorpe. No one will forget his ever-winning black boy, Mr. Successful, a top winner in Canada and finished in the States by Tom Campbell. Denzil lives in St. Thomas, Ontario.

The Playboys of the Toronto area exhibit their lovely partis and attend numerous shows with a nice string of Cockers for their many clients.

The name Jayvana, though reasonably new to Cockers, is making a name in both countries, with Joan Van Doornick showing her pretty buff girls and now handling for others.

We see chocolates of the Bill Greenwoods (Salsam); the pretty blacks and black and tans of Canbream, and the partis of Duffville. Some new names to watch will be Dublin, Carbert, Glendorgal, and too many others to mention, but all sincere breeders.

There are a few limited specialty shows in Canada each year. They get top American judges and are well supported by both Canadian and U.S. exhibitors. There are several Cocker boosters held in conjunction with the all-breed shows.

If you think Canada is far behind, you are in for a surprise. Many of the breeders are showing their own in the States and are winning. No longer is it easy to put on a Canadian title either. There must be competition for a point and remember, there are *four* varieties (black and tans are shown in a class to themselves) and only ONE Cocker goes into the group.

There is no height disqualification but the breeders have themselves kept the size down. They have had and do have the same problems, but they are meeting these head on. Eye clinics are set up and many are able to go to the States to the clinics as well. One could say much for the "old days". There were larger classes. Often twenty or more black males at the all-breed shows but the quality now far surpasses what has been lost in larger classes, and that is what the breeders are striving to attain.

It has been the good lines from the States that have helped to improve the Cocker Spaniel in Canada, but it has been the work and determination of the Canadian breeders to carry on that has helped to establish their own good lines.

Am. & Can. Ch. Bun-Al's Fortune Cookie, top American Cocker (bitch) all varieties in Canada for 1975; top Cocker for British Columbia 1973, 1974, 1975.

The Cocker Spaniel in Western Canada
by Maxine Norris

The American Cocker in Western Canada, particularly British Columbia, goes back many years, although most of the breeders of the 1940s and '50s are no longer active. Our Norwyn Kennels are still active having started in Cockers in 1954 with buffs of Stockdale line and breeding these into the Norbill line.

The buffs were nice, but the more we saw the partis, the more interested we became. In 1959, a black and v hite bitch puppy was

161

purchased from Jim and Beth Hall of Hall-Way fame. Her name was Canadian Champion Hall-Way Hoodwinked, sired by Ch. Mestler's Extra Special out of Ch. Hall-Way Honey Hue, a half sister of the great Ch. Hall-Way Hoot Mon.

Hoodwinked became the foundation of the Norwyn parti-colors. One of her sons, the red and white Can. Ch. Norwyn's Nortorious, born in 1960 and sired by Norbill's High & Mighty, was one of the most beautiful dogs we ever bred. Nortorious won his first Group at 10 months of age and went on to many wonderful wins. He also proved his worth as a sire with many champion children and grandchildren. Norwyn bitches were bred out to dogs such as Ch. Hall-Way Hoot Mon, Ch. Hall-Way Hard Tri, Ch. Camby's Contribution, Ch. Dreamridge Domino and Dreamridge Dan Cupid.

The purchase of the red and white male Can. Ch. Regalia's Donovan in 1972, a Ch. Regalia's Snowdrifter and Rexpointe Muriel son, brought in new blood and super showmanship. Donovan is the double grandsire of Can. Ch. Norwyn's Patrick O'Donovan and sire of Can. Ch. Norwyn's Miss Congeniality, Can. Ch. Norwyn's Nonstop, Can. Ch. Norwyn's Parti Pooper, Can. Ch. Bun-Al's Dancing Doll, Can. Ch. Bun-Al's Dancing Master, American and Canadian Ch. Westland's Lord Tri-Don and Can. Ch. Barona's Cinnamon Twist. He has several more pointed offspring and some lovely looking babies waiting their turn in the showring.

Hec Norris, my husband, was one of the Canadians licensed as a handler by the AKC and he handles all of the Norwyn dogs. Our Cockers have been sold to several countries including Holland, Switzerland and Venezuela.

We are also the founders of the British Columbia Cocker Spaniel Club organized in 1959. The Club consists of breeders and fanciers of both American and British Cockers and a Specialty show for both breeds is held each year in April, attracting entries from British Columbia, Alberta and the United States.

Another very active British Columbia breeder is Al Richardson and his wife Bunny with the Bunn-Al Cockers. They are the breeders of the top winning red and white bitch, Ch. Bun-Al's Niki Nightingale. The Richardsons also breed blacks, mostly of Flo-Bob background.

Diane and Chuck Lilley (Timothy) stopped showing actively for a while but are now back in the show ring with some lovely blacks such as American and Canadian Ch. Timothy's Holy Moses and a couple of very nice young black and tans. Some of their breeding is behind the top winning bitch American and Canadian Ch. Tabaka's Tidbit O'Wynden.

Des and Rene Gillis of Desersne's Kennels, Dandy and Harry Von Czarnowski of Wig-Wag Kennels, Ruth and Dave Jones of Karlyle Kennels are other successful active breeders.

Two new breeders are Gord and Sue Stich of Prince George, B.C., and Mr. and Mrs. Ronald Robert of Williams Lake, B.C.

I believe this covers most of the active breeders in Western Canada; if I have overlooked some, please accept my apologies.

Over the years, I have seen the stock improve tremendously. It keeps getting better all the time and competition gets tougher and tougher for everybody. This is a good thing and shows the breeders what a lot of thinking before breeding will do. I know that for myself the past years have been full of excitement, heartaches and downright hard work, but I would not have wanted it any other way.

Show Champion Bullen Whisky Galore, Best of Breed and Reserve Best in Gundog Group at Crufts 1977. Owned by Andrew and Muriel Caine, Nottingham, England.

C.C. winners, England. Left, Am. & Eng. Show Ch. Sundust Bleuaire Repercussion. Right, Ch. Dreamridge Delegate.

7

The American Cocker in Other Countries

Great Britain
by Muriel and Andrew Caine (Trotwell, Notts, England)

The first show type American Cocker was imported into England in 1965, but there is no doubt there were several previous to this brought over by your servicemen and countrymen. Certainly one black male brought over during the war by an officer in the U.S.A.F., spent a considerable time with a prominent Terrier breeder in Sheffield. However, it was not until June 1967, that the parent Club, The American Cocker Club of Great Britain, took its first steps as a ruling body, and many more dogs became available, either through breeding or import. Starting with a handful of dedicated breeders, most of whom bred Cocker Spaniels—English variety, pioneers of breedings and importation, we now in 1977 have approximately 130 members who regularly exhibit. Registrations over the past ten years have been gradually increasing from a yearly number of 250 plus, to last year's more than 500. Most of us are rather horrified at this staggering increase, as at the last championship show held by the parent Club, the total entry was 128 exhibits: 62 dogs, 66 bitches; and this was a record. The usual entry at any championship show is about 70.

There has been a marked increase in the number of commercial pet breeders who think nothing of buying and selling half a dozen brood bitches (usually under 18 months) at a time. This is really bad, as there is still not sufficient good quality stock. There are several very good dogs, but the bitches still need improvement on the whole. Great concern has been felt over the incidence of cataract which is numerically considerable. The Club has tried very hard to encourage new breeders to take advantage of the Kennel Club British Veterinarian Association Scheme. Test mating has taken place under prominent veterinary supervision, but with little or no conclusions as to the cause and or effect. Most of us now test regularly our breeding stock to registered B.V.A. vets, with a permanent certificate being issued at five years, an interim at three years. Many of us do not breed stock or offer dogs at stud until three years old, but it is certainly a hardship to wait this long for someone just coming into the breed.

There is a rescue scheme associated with the Parent Club, which has proved most successful in finding suitable, loving homes for the less fortunate of our lovely breed. No pedigrees are given, and all bitches are spayed. This service is done by committee members and funds are raised, both for the effort and the cataract scheme, at most of our club shows.

Early 1970 saw the formation of the Northern Counties American Cocker Club. Northern members of our Club felt that, though they would still support the parent Club, travelings and the doubling of ideas would considerably help our lovely breed. This year, they are to hold their own first Championship Show to be judged by Dr. Adolfo Spector from the Argentine, who has been over to England on numerous occasions, and indeed has judged one of our own club's early shows.

The American Cocker Spaniel Club of Great Britian has held two open shows each year with 16 classes. There are usually between 40 and 50 dogs at these events. For the last four years, the Kennel Club has granted us Championship Status. It may not be generally known by the American exhibitors that in England we do not have color classes, nor do we have a point system. We do not have color champions; only one dog and one bitch go forward at the championship show for the Challenge Certificate. This makes for much harder wins.

There are 26 all-breed shows held in Great Britain annually plus one in Belfast, plus one Breed Club. There are now 22 sets of CCs for the American Cocker.

Since 1970, when CCs were first offered for the breed, to the time of writing, 31 champions have been made; 16 blacks, 5 partis, 8 black and tans, and 2 buffs.

In 1972, came the announcement from the Kennel Club that they were proposing to regroup the American into the Utility Group as they did not consider they could work carrying so much coat, and were therefore more a glamour dog. This caused great consternation by the dedicated breeders and club members as a whole. Many friends in other breeds took up the challenge with us. In July, 1972, a delegation from the ACSC of Great Britain armed with a petition and signatures numbering hundreds went to the Kennel Club in London to try to persuade them not to allow this to happen.

In this same 1972, a Delegate red and white son passed his working test and another breeder trained two of his show champion bitches in the field to take their full championship.

It was with great relief that by Spring 1974 we had the welcome news from the Kennel Club that they would be pleased to allow us to remain in the Gun Dog group provided we adapted the coat length and quantity. Hence, the fact is that our dogs carry less coat than their relatives in the U.S.A.

We find these lovely little dogs are becoming very popular, and do hold their own very effectively at all types of shows. Very many Best Puppy and Best in Show awards can be credited to their honor.

The top winning American of all time here, of course, is Am. Ch. and Sh. Ch. Dreamridge Delegate. He took so many Best of Breeds I have lost count, but certainly he has 15 CCs and 8 Reserve CCs. He is the only one to win Best in Show and Reserve Best in Show at an all-breed championship show. He is now retired, but has seven group wins including Crufts, 1972; Gun Dog of the Year, 1971, (all Gun Dogs); and Best American Cocker, 1971, '72, '73. He won 30 Bests in Show altogether and is one of the top sires in the breed.

Apart from siring many winners here and overseas, he is sire of my Sh. Ch. Whisky Galore, winner of two Groups, two Reserve Groups (one Reserve being Crufts), and Best in Show at both Championship Shows, 1976, where he became the first red and white American Champion. He now has 11 CCs and is still only $2\frac{1}{2}$ years old. He was American of the year in 1976.

The litter of nine pups which contained this lovely boy was from a granddaughter-grandfather mating which has become one of the great litters. In it there are: one English Sh. Ch. Group Winner, one English CC and Reserve CC Winner, one Sh. African Ch. and Best in Show and Group Winner, one New Zealand Champion and one CC Winner in Switzerland. The only other red and white to win any prominence was my Ch. Mittina Tiger's Tail, the first red and white to score top honors, winning a Reserve CC under an American judge, Mr. J.

167

Warwick. He won many Best Puppy and Bests in Show and a Junior Warrant. He was by Delegate out of my imported black and white bitch's daughter Ballantrae Dreamawhile. Tiger's Tail was exported to Australia in 1972.

We look forward to more progress in the breed, as a whole here in Great Britain, as we think the Cocker the best all-around dog for most people.

The Cocker Spaniel in Holland
by Marilyn W. Pryor

Following World War II, the Cocker Spaniel, American type, began to be seen in Europe. The first American Cockers to be exhibited in Holland were two Black and Tans that were shown at the Royal Holland Kennel Club's Winners Show in Amsterdam in 1948. Since the Federation Cynologic International did not recognize the American Cocker as a separate breed, these two were shown in the classes for English Cocker Spaniels, and quite naturally, did no winning. However, at this show, these new Spaniels were seen by Mrs. Nell Koning-Goudappel of Naarden, and she became enchanted with this smaller type of Cocker Spaniel. Mrs. Koning had been a breeder of English Cocker Spaniels, and in 1949 while on a trip to Germany she met American officers who had the Cocker Spaniels, and had an opportunity to buy a puppy out of the Blairwood breeding. This particular puppy did not live to adulthood, but in 1951, Mrs. Koning returned to Germany and bought another bitch of the same breeding, Jane of Herzogtum Julich (by Ch. Blairwood Broomstraw ex Blairwood Broom Miss). Mrs. Koning asked the Federation Cynologic International for recognition of this breed; it was granted, and thus, Jane (a golden buff) became the first American Cocker Spaniel to be judged as a separate breed in Europe. Jane had a lovely show career and as Mrs. Koning notes, why not? She was the only one! Jane was bred to her sire, Ch. Blairwood Broomstraw, and the resulting litter of five produced one Champion (Dutch), Buffer Boy of the Cockerbox. The Cockerbox (der Cockerbox) has become Mrs. Koning's well known kennel name.

In 1954, Mrs. Koning imported from the United States, Blue Bay's Come and Get It, a black dog. His name was prophetic as he easily won his Dutch, German, Belgium and World Championship titles. In 1958, Come and Get It was Reserve Best in Show at the Hague, defeating over 900 dogs. About a year later, Mrs. Koning again turned to the United States, this time for a bitch, and brought Qualine's Count

first American Cocker Spaniel ported to Holland and Europe n the U.S. (1954): Ch. Blue 's Come and Get It, owned by l Koning. (Picture unre- ched, taken in field trial.)

Second Best in Show, Amsterdam, 1968. Ch. Pryority's Presentation. Handled by Ron Fabis.

Me In to Holland. It appears that this bitch and Come And Get It became the foundation of the breed in Holland, appearing on about 80% of the pedigrees in the country. Together they produced six champions.

As these two were producing well in the years 1950-56, it became obvious that new lines were necessary for the progeny of these dogs. Mrs. Koning imported a lovely black and tan Fancy Parade son, Pinetop's Fancy Dutchman. The champion daughters of Come And Get It and Count Me In are: Ch. Lady Be Good of the Cockerbox, Ch. Notice Me of the Cockerbox, German Ch. Favorite Miss of the Cockerbox, and Ch. Miss Independence of the Cockerbox. They were bred to Fancy Dutchman and produced a great number of good American Cocker Spaniels. Fancy Dutchman himself had an illustrious show career being a Group winner and winning 12 Bests of Breed (i.e. BOV).

To this point, Mrs. Koning was, indeed, a pioneer in the promotion of the American Cocker Spaniel in Holland, and quite naturally, she was not receiving great cooperation from the English Cocker Spaniel Club, of which she was a member. In 1964, Mrs. Koning asked the Dutch Kennel Club for permission to form the American Cocker Spaniel Club of the Netherlands, and this Club, the first for American Cocker Spaniels in Europe, began with but 20 members.

Once again, in 1963, Mrs. Koning imported a lovely black dog, Ch. Merrywag's Bit O'Luck purchased from Ann Brojanac of Valli-Lo Kennels. In April of 1967, Ann and John Brojanac were in Holland visiting Mrs. Koning and they attended the Dog Show in s'Hertogenbosch, a town about 50 miles from Amsterdam. In an entry of 11 American Cockers, Mrs. Koning's black bitch, Dutch Champion Touchy Toy of Gerwy's Home won Best of Breed, and then went on to top the Non-Continental Gun Dog Group, and on to the ultimate, Best in Show; the first time an American Cocker Spaniel had won a Best in Show at an FCI show in Europe! What a thrill for the Brojanacs to witness this triumph of the breed!

Ch. Valli-Lo's Vagabond (buff) and Valli-Lo's Bon Voyage (black bitch) followed Bit O'Luck to Holland where both had successful ring careers between 1964 and 1970. Vagabond, by Ch. Kahola's Keystone ex Ch. Valli-Lo's Vicuna, was never defeated and won 18 Bests of Variety, 3 Group firsts and 5 other Group placings. Bon Voyage was a top winning bitch in Holland and produced 3 champion daughters. In 1969, Mrs. Koning imported Ch. Rob-Mar's Gold Rush, a dog helpful in improving neck and shoulders and giving length of neck.

Finally, the American Cocker Spaniel was catching on, and Mrs. Koning was no longer alone in the promotion of the breed. Others began to import and to breed good specimens and today, the American Cocker Spaniel Club of the Netherlands has over 330 members. In the '60s and '70s, dogs from Juniper, Vango, Pryority, Alorah, Laurim, Dreamridge, Blue Bay, and Harlanhaven joined the earlier imports to add strength and diversity to the breed. It is interesting to note that the number of American Cocker Spaniel puppies registered in the Dutch Kennel Club Yearbook (*Raad Van Beheer op Kynologisch Gebied in Nederland*) has risen from 21 in 1957 to 737 in 1976.

In addition to Mrs. Koning, many Dutch breeders have been involved in breeding better American Cockers in Holland. They include: Mr. ten Cate, Mrs. Will de Vries-Hoogland, Mr. v. Maris, Mrs. Truus Holslag v. Sensus, Mrs. Muller, Mrs. Lüte, Mrs. de Wit, Mrs. v. d. Meuleb, Mrs. Stooten, and Mrs. Lagerveld.

These dedicated Dutch breeders are also following the United States in using eye tests for their breeding stock. Since late in 1976, an eye clinic has been established in Utrecht under Dr. F. C. Stades, and animals may be tested from 18 months old for various hereditary eye diseases.

The quality of the American Cocker Spaniel in Holland is high, and with continued dedication on the part of those actively breeding, the future of the American Cocker is bright in the land of canals, tulips, and windmills.

The Cocker Spaniel in France
by Marilyn W. Pryor

In turning our attention to France, we find that, once again, it is an English Cocker Spaniel breeder who found the smaller Cocker Spaniels pleasing to her and became the mentor of the breed. In France it was Mme. Françoise Firminhac.

The Spaniel Club Français was founded in 1898 as the parent Club for Sporting Spaniels (*Épagneuls de chasse*), and the first American Cockers to be registered in the French Stud Book in 1957 were owned by Col. Shiras Blair. These two Black and Tans were shown at the Paris show in March of 1957. Mme. Firminhac had seen pictures of American Cockers in American breed magazines, and she was very impressed with them. In February of 1958, her first two American Cockers arrived from the Biggs' kennel in the U.S.; a silver buff dog, Biggs' My Silver Prince, and a black bitch, Biggs' Promise (Ch. Biggs' Eager Beaver ex Biggs' Platinum Doll). These two imports were shown at the Paris show in 1959 and became the number three and number four American Cockers registered in the French Stud Book.

Mme. Francoise Firminhac
of Lommoye, France.

These American imports were not particularly welcomed by breeders of Cocker Spaniels, and it was believed that they could not compete with the English Cocker Spaniels in popularity. Mme. Firminhac was alone in exhibiting "*les Americains*," as Mrs. Koning had been in Holland. However, she feels that Promise did much to introduce the French fancy to the breed. Promise was a very showy bitch with a lovely character, and she became a Group winner. She retired at age five, undefeated in the breed.

Promise produced three litters by Silver Prince, and from the first litter Mme. Firminhac retained a lovely, light buff bitch, Ivory Pimpernell de la Haulte Fortelle. Mrs. Biggs continued to counsel Mme. Firminhac, who went on to breed some very good Cocker Spaniels under the "Haulte Fortelle" name, dogs that were recognized in France and throughout Europe. In 1961, Biggs' Mister Pepys, a silver buff dog came to Mme. Firminhac. He became Champion of France and Luxembourg, and International Champion. Bred to Ivory Pimpernell, he produced multiple champion litters.

Another import, Biggs' Snow Frolic, a silver buff bitch, was shown to her French, Italian, Monocan, and International titles in 1965. Bred

172

to Pepys, she established a line of buffs and silvers that is still considered one of the best on the continent. A daughter of Frolic, Quelle Belle Pompadour de la Haulte Fortelle, bred to different males, produced five bitch champions.

Also in 1965, Mme. Firminhac imported Ch. Pinefair Parson, a black dog. He was shown to his French, Italian, Monocan, and Iternational championships. Then, bred to Pimpernell, he produced Panache de la Haulte Fortelle who was one of the top winning and top producing Cockers in France in the 1960s. Once more turning to the Biggs, who had been so helpful to her in the past, Mme. Firminhac imported Biggs' Gay Cavalier in 1968. This dog proved helpful in head improvement in the silvers and buffs, especially when bred to Pompadour. He was shown to his French and Italian titles, and he produced six champions.

In 1975, Mme. Firminhac turned to another respected American kennel for Harlanhaven Hemingway, a silver buff, who in just 13 months gained his French, Monocan, and Spanish championships. Hemingway, in addition to producing heavily coated buffs and silvers, also produces brightly marked Black and Tans with a good coat factor.

While Mme. Firminhac was alone for many years in her breeding and showing of American Cockers, she began to be joined along the way by other admirers of this smaller Cocker Spaniel. In 1963, Mme. Monique Rufer bought a pet Cocker from the Haulte Fortelle Kennel, and she began to put together a breeding program of her own. In 1971, Mme. Rufer bought Can. Ch. Twinhaven Kelly the Kid, a tri-color dog. He became French and International Champion, and was also a good producer. In 1972, Can. Ch. Nirvana Farm's Can Can Girl joined the dogs at Mme. Rufer's kennel. By this time, her "of Merrily" suffix was being known in the fancy. 1974 saw Am. and Mex. Ch. Windridge Chocolate Baron arrive at Mme. Rufer's and in 1976, Windridge Jonquil, a buff bitch, joined him. Mme. Rufer and her friend, Mrs. Margaret Newton of Germany, were interested in the chocolate color and in 1976 they imported BeGay's Phillip S. Hershey who is currently being shown. It should be noted that the chocolates in France are shown in the Parti-color variety.

Mme. Guerville-Sevin, who is Secretary of the Spaniel Club Français, in 1966 bought Ch. Phyllis (a littermate to Panache) and subsequently bred her to Biggs' Gay Cavalier with the resulting litter being of show quality.

Also in 1966, another littermate of Panache, Paprika, was bought by Mme. de Montmollin of the kennel "de Valangin," and he was used successfully with bitches in both France and Germany.

173

Left: **Int. and Fr. Ch. Van Gogh Philandra de la Baia, bred in France, 1972, by Mme. Yvette Kapfer** Owned by **M. Philippe Neraud.** Right: **Ch. Qualine's Count Me In, foundation bitch of the Dut** **American Cockers. Owned by Mrs. Nell Koning.**

Mme. Helêne Pashaus bought Ravishing Princess of Merrily from Mme. Rufer in 1968. This black bitch was by Ch. Pinefair Parson ex Look Me Over of the Cockerbox. Mme. Pashaus became interested in Parti-colors and imported Fi-Fo's Focus from the United States. This tri-colored bitch was bred to Twinhaven's Kelly the Kid and produced several tri-colored litters. This was the first time tri-colors had been bred in France. A bitch from the first litter, bearing Mme. Pashaus kennel name, Isoline de la Pasaudiere, has had remarkable success in the ring.

And, in 1971, Mme. Bergier, using the kennel name "de Valembreuse," began a breeding program with the purchase of Puff Powder de la Haulte Fortelle (Ch. Biggs' Gay Cavalier ex Pompadour de la

Haulte Fortelle). This bitch was bred to a buff dog, Sanstar Continental Trooper, imported from Canada, and the resulting puppies were the lightest silvers to be seen in France.

In 1966, Mme. Yvette Kapferer bought a buff dog and a buff bitch from Mrs. Koning in Holland, and showed them to their French Championships. In late 1968, she purchased two Black and Tans from the United States to be the foundation for her Black and Tan breeding program: Ch. Pryority's Presentation and Ch. Phi Tau's Sugarfoot. At the Royal Holland Kennel Club Winners Show in Amsterdam in 1968, Mme. Kapferer was present to see her new import, Presentation, win Best of Breed, Best Non-Continental Gun Dog, and Reserve Best in Show in his continental ring debut in an entry of 2310 dogs. Mme. Kapferer later imported a Parti-color, Just Plain War Bonnet, and in 1972 she bought Pett's Viscount, a buff dog, Pryority's Vamp de la Philandra de la Baia, a buff bitch, and Pryority's Passport, a brightly marked Black and Tan (Ch. Laynewood Lancer ex Ch. Pryority's Parisienne). Passport became a French and International Champion, and, in 1976, gave Mme. Kapferer quite a thrill by winning Best in Show at the prestigious "Bouafles," all Sporting Spaniel Show.

In 1973, a young man named Philippe Neraud came to Mme. Kapferer's kennel, Philandra de la Baia in Missillac, to buy a dog. This he did, a lovely black male: Van Gogh Philandra de la Baia (Pryority's Passport ex Int. Ch. Kildeholm's Funny Face). M. Neraud gave Van Gogh a fine ring career, finishing him to both his French and International titles with many excellent wins along the way. M. Neraud made a trip to the United States in 1974 when he bought Pryority's Pleasant Trip, a black bitch that has in turn produced several fine puppies for him. He later acquired Ch. Pryority's Promise Me (Ch. Rinky Dink's Sir Lancelot ex Ch. Pryority's Promises Promises). This bitch completed her French Championship in just three shows, including, of course, winning at the Paris show which is a necessity to wear the French crown. M. Neraud later bought Nor-Mar's News in the Night from the kennels of Mari and Norman Doty. M. Neraud continues to breed under the kennel name, Black Magic.

Under the thoughtful auspices of the Spaniel Club Français, and with the continued dedication of French breeders as mentioned here, the American Cocker Spaniel in France is making excellent progress. In 1969, only 356 American Cocker Spaniels were registered in the French Stud Book. Today, there are more than 600 registered and the number is growing. Could this affection shown our merry, little Cocker by the French fancy be based on a mutual *joie d'vivre?*

The Cocker Spaniel in Mexico
by Owen L. Young

Mexico has had a colorful history in breeding and showing the American Cocker Spaniel. Some of the original breeders' stock goes back to Stockdale and other older American kennels. Senora Joan Moreno and her husband Jose had dogs from Stockdale Kennels in the late 1940s and early '50s. Other Cocker breeders have been Elena de la Gorza, and Doctor Roberto Hernandez Avalos. These are currently principal breeders of the American Cocker Spaniel.

Some of the American Cocker Spaniel owners registered in Mexico are: Criadero de la Mancha, R. F. Fitzsimmons, Alec Gonzales, Elena Schulse, Criadero San Walvor, Senor Jorge Chaim Bravo, Senor Rafael Serrano, Senor Gary N. Chaffee, Senora Gloria M. De Aigster, Sr. Fidel Gutierrez Solana, Sr. Enrique Fernandez del Busto, Sra. Estela Monzon de Wolf, Dr. Lorenzo Roca Ferrer, Ing. Emilk Michner, Sr. Melvin T. Olans, Lidia Van Der Meerr, Sra. Ilse W. de Clasen, Sr. Angel Sotres Moriega, Sra. Anne Hill de Mayagoitia, Sr. Ignacio Murguia Castellanos, Sra. Ma. Antoinieta G. de Gomar, Criadero Tangamanga's, Sra. Dora Conzalez Rubio, Arq. Enrique Henonin y Sra, and Sr. Gabriel R. Marzuez Agras.

The Cocker Delegation in Mexico is one of the major divisions of *Asociacion Canofila Mexicana* and one of its major assets because it is one of the oldest. Since approximately 1967, the Delegation has given a Specialty Show each year and has bought, owned, and bred many fine dogs. There is a tremendous interest in the Cocker Spaniel in Mexico and the entries at the all-breed shows generally are among the largest. In 1976, about 500 American Cocker Spaniels were shown in Mexico.

Some of the current Best in Show winners in Mexico are Am. and Mex. Ch. Silver Maple's Early Return, and Am. and Mex. Ch. Delphi's Warlock. Some of its highest winners are Am. and Mex. Ch. Tamburlaines' Evel Knievel, Am. and Mex. Ch. Ran Wal's Lookout and Mex. Ch. Delphi's Tabatha Key. Some of the leading winners are Mex. Ch. Kekko's Chosin, Mex. Ch. Tu-Jan's Tar and Feather, and Mex. Ch. Tu-Jan's Fedora. Other Best in Show Winners are Am. and Mex. Champion Normar's Nameplate, and Mex. Ch. Lucanos.

Mexicans are working diligently to improve the breed, both from their own breeding programs and from the stock which they import. They, along with the Columbians and the Venezuelans, have been endeavoring to have Federation Cynologique Internationale recognize the three varieties separately for International points. This program is

Ch. Kekko's Daikoku of Willowood, buff whelped 1971, is an American, Mexican, Canadian and Venezuelan champion. Owned by Dr. Owen L. Young.

Best in Show in Mexico: Am. & Mex. Ch. Silver Maple Early Return, owned by Senora Joan Moreno.

still under way and, hopefully, will be attained in 1977 or 1978 with the assistance of Senora Thelma VonThaden of Mexico.

The Cocker Spaniel in South America
by Owen L. Young

In Colombia, the most prominent Cocker breeders at the moment are Harrald and Josephine Barth, who have lined up a good foundation in all three varieties and are currently showing International Champion LaMar's Luxury, a lovely Best in Show bitch.

Cockers, in the past, have been owned and promoted to Best in Show by German Garcia and also Eduardo Vargas, who currently has a black Best in Show bitch.

Argentina is strong in showing top quality Cockers and is continually buying some of the best American Cockers for showing and breeding.

Brazil has a large number of Cocker breeders and a Specialty every year. Cocker entries in the shows present a good representation of the breed. Several Brazilians are currently members of the American Spaniel Club.

The largest Cocker breeders in Venezuela are Senor and Senora Osuna. Senor and Senora Francisco Virgili also breed Cockers. Venezuela is strong in Blacks and Parti Colors. One of the outstanding handlers and judges of the American Cocker Spaniel in South America is Richard Guevera, who judges on all continents. Champion Dreamridge Demijohn is one of the current Best in Show International Champion American Cocker Spaniels.

Interest in the Cocker Spaniel is rapidly accelerating throughout the world, but most particularly in Central and South America.

One of the problems is the difficulty that foreign breeders have in getting quality showing and breeding stock. They are willing to pay excellent prices and are often charged these excellent prices and shipped poor pet quality animals. They buy the puppy because of the sire or the dam or the kennel name behind the dog or the bitch.

The American Cocker Spaniel in Japan
by Mikio Takanashi

In the early 1950s, Walt Disney's fantastic cartoon movie, "The Lady and the Tramp," featuring a buff Cocker bitch, scored a great success all over Japan. This was the incentive for a Cocker boom in Japan, lasting over ten years.

178

Mexican Champion Kekko's Kuroi Choshin, owned by Dr. Owen Young.

Mexican Champion Kekko's Komidori, Best of Breed, International Winter Circuit. Bred and owned by Dr. Owen Young. Handled by Dee Dee Wood.

Int. & Venez. Ch. Kekko's Haru-No-Hana, black bitch, Best of Breed, Group 3rd winner. Bred and owned by Dr. Owen Young. Handled by Thomas A. Duncan.

Cockers placing 1, 2 and 4 in Sporting Group at Association Canina de Caracas 1973 under American judge Dr. Frank Booth. Left to right, Int. Ch. Glenmeadow Great Guns, Int & Am. Ch. Dreamridge Decorator and Int. and Am. Ch. Kekko's Daikoku of Willowood, handled respectively by Richard Guevara, Carmen Osuna and Thomas Duncan.

The heroine completely charmed most people who enjoyed the film with her lovely eyes and funny long ears. Women and children became Cocker fans. As soon as they got out of the theater, they rushed to pet shops.

People were satisfied if they could buy a dog with long ears and a fluffy coat. Most did not pay attention to the quality of the dog. The breed soon became the recommended item of pet shop unions and they executed mass-merchandising in cooperation with backyard kennels.

Of course, the breed was in Japan before the boom. Some of them came from the States as pets of American families to Japan and others were imported. Among them, we can find the name of popular kennels, i.e., Ch. Countryside Carousel Spookie and Stockdale Arnold. These two contributed to our breeding program at this period.

Thus, the first stage for the Cocker in Japan opened its curtain.

During the 1950s and early 1960s, Cocker Spaniel popularity was on a steady upswing, growing year by year. In 1962, over 12,000 Cockers were registered with the Japan Kennel Club, and the breed was positioned in the top five breeds in the registration race.

Population of Cockers today has unfortunately declined. From April 1976 to March 1977 registrations totaled only 1561, number 17 in ranking. Maltese enjoyed the number one ranking, registering 31,866 for this period. Two reasons given for the decline are that the breed needs heavy grooming and that the breed has suffered in character due to random breeding and poor stud and foundation forces.

Contrary to these facts, truly sincere breeders and exhibitors of the breed have been growing year by year. The N.C.S.K. (Japan Cocker Spaniel Association, Inc.), founded in 1962, is one evidence of this serious interest.

Very important to the fanciers of American Cockers is that there is no separation of the three colors.

In 1973, a third kennel club named Kennel Club of Japan was established. They offer another all breed registration other than that of the Japan Kennel Club. Thus, we have three ways to register Cockers.

There are three stages open to us in Japan for showing a Cocker Spaniel, since there are three kennel Clubs offering registration services. Among exhibitors, some show their dogs in the three clubs, while others are faithful to one organization.

Anyhow, shows are always our main excitement. Here, I would like to describe the system of shows in Japan:

Shows: Since the J.K.C. has a long history of almost thirty years, they organize their area clubs nationwide and hold their shows for all

181

Japanese dogs ready for the show ring.

American Cockers being shown at a Japanese dog show, 1976.

breeds and specialties about 200 times a year, enjoying big entries. In all breed shows, entries are classified in the following Groups: Group one, Japan's original dogs; Group two, Working dogs; Group three, Sporting dogs; Group four, Hound dogs; Group five, Terriers; Group six, Toy dogs; Group seven, Non-Sporting dogs.

K.C. of Japan Shows: This organization was started only four years ago by the persons who were unhappy in J.K.C., both professional and amateur. Champion titles are given when a dog gets a total of ten points, including two major points from two different judges. In specialty shows, the following three classes are added: breeder-owner, novice, and foreign. ·

N.C.S.K. Specialty Show: This organization seems to be patterned after the American Spaniel Club. N.C.S.K. is constructed of 11 regional Cocker Spaniel Clubs. Each Cocker Spaniel Club holds specialty shows and other regional activities while the mother club, N.C.S.K., holds an annual national specialty show in the same fashion as the ASC National Specialty.

They have an independent registration system which closely resembles the AKC's. They recognize three varieties and the class entry system is strictly similar to the one in the States. Although the scale of the club is small, the members are proud of being top grade Cocker fanciers in Japan.

The improvement of the Cocker in Japan has been dependent upon dogs and bitches imported from the States, the origin of the breed. Over the last twenty years, a hundred dogs and bitches were imported, most of them were champion titled, and these have been the main stud dogs and foundation bitches. Frankly, very few Japanese kennels have contributed to Cocker bloodlines in Japan. We have a few good domestic forces for breeding, but also Cockers that are of no use for this purpose. For the sake of our beloved breed, we would like to import more good Cockers from the States. We hope that those shipping a Cocker to Japan will send the highest quality dogs, to help us further good breeding.

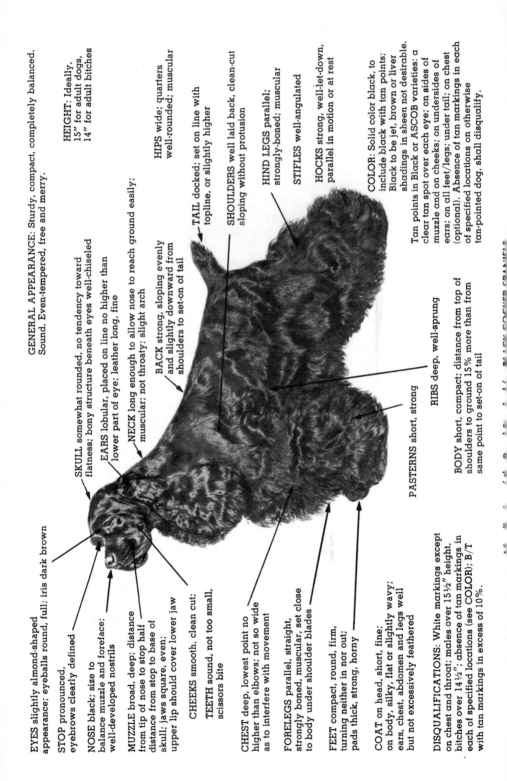

GENERAL APPEARANCE: Sturdy, compact, completely balanced. Sound. Even-tempered, free and merry.

HEIGHT: Ideally, 15" for adult dogs, 14" for adult bitches

HIPS wide: quarters well-rounded; muscular

TAIL docked; set on line with topline, or slightly higher

SHOULDERS well laid back, clean-cut sloping without protusion

HIND LEGS parallel; strongly-boned; muscular

STIFLES well-angulated

HOCKS strong, well-let-down, parallel in motion or at rest

COLOR: Solid color black, to include black with tan points: Black to be jet, brown or liver shadings in sheen not desirable. Tan points in Black or ASCOB varieties: a clear tan spot over each eye; on sides of muzzle and on cheeks; on undersides of ears; on all feet/legs; under tail; on chest (optional). Absence of tan markings in each of specified locations on otherwise tan-pointed dog, shall disqualify.

SKULL somewhat rounded, no tendency toward flatness; bony structure beneath eyes well-chiseled

EARS lobular, placed on line no higher than lower part of eye; leather long, fine

NECK long enough to allow nose to reach ground easily; muscular; not throaty; slight arch

BACK strong, sloping evenly and slightly downward from shoulders to set-on of tail

RIBS deep, well-sprung

BODY short, compact; distance from top of shoulders to ground 15% more than from same point to set-on of tail

PASTERNS short, strong

EYES slightly almond-shaped appearance; eyeballs round, full; iris dark brown

STOP pronounced, eyebrows clearly defined

NOSE black; size to balance muzzle and foreface; well-developed nostrils

MUZZLE broad, deep: distance from tip of nose to stop half distance from stop to base of skull; jaws square, even; upper lip should cover lower jaw

CHEEKS smooth, clean cut;

TEETH sound, not too small, scissors bite

CHEST deep, lowest point no higher than elbows: not so wide as to interfere with movement

FORELEGS parallel, straight, strongly boned, muscular, set close to body under shoulder blades

FEET compact, round, firm, turning neither in nor out; pads thick, strong, horny

COAT on head, short, fine; on body, silky, flat or slightly wavy: ears, chest, abdomen and legs well but not excessively feathered

DISQUALIFICATIONS: White markings except on chest and throat; males over 15½" height. bitches over 14½"; absence of tan markings in each of specified locations (see COLOR); B/T with tan markings in excess of 10%.

8

Official AKC Standard for the Cocker Spaniel

General Appearance—The Cocker Spaniel is the smallest member of the Sporting Group. He has a sturdy, compact body and a cleanly chiseled and refined head, with the overall dog in complete balance and of ideal size. He stands well up at the shoulder on straight forelegs with a topline sloping slightly toward strong, muscular quarters. He is a dog capable of considerable speed, combined with great endurance. Above all he must be free and merry, sound, well balanced throughout, and in action show a keen inclination to work; equable in temperament with no suggestion of timidity.

Head—To attain a well-proportioned head, which must be in balance with the rest of the dog, it embodies the following:

Skull—Rounded but not exaggerated with no tendency toward flatness; the eyebrows are clearly defined with a pronounced stop. The bony structure beneath the eyes is well chiseled with no prominence in the cheeks.

Muzzle—Broad and deep, with square, even jaws. The upper lip is full and of sufficient depth to cover the lower jaw. To be in correct balance, the distance from the stop to the tip of the nose is one half the distance from the stop up over the crown to the base of the skull.

Teeth—Strong and sound, not too small, and meet in a scissors bite.

Nose—Of sufficient size to balance the muzzle and foreface, with well-developed nostrils typical of a sporting dog. It is black in color in the blacks and black and tans. In other colors it may be brown, liver or black, the darker the better. The color of the nose harmonizes with the color of the eye rim.

GENERAL APPEARANCE: Sturdy, compact, completely balanced. Sound. Even-tempered, free and merry.

EYES slightly almond-shaped appearance; eyeballs round, full; iris dark brown

STOP pronounced; eyebrows clearly defined

NOSE size to balance muzzle and foreface; well-developed nostrils.

MUZZLE broad, deep; distance from tip of nose to stop is half that from stop to base of skull; jaws square, even; upper lip should cover lower jaw

CHEEKS smooth, clean cut;

TEETH sound, not too small, scissors bite

SHOULDERS well laid back; clean-cut, sloping without protusion

CHEST deep, lowest point no higher than elbows; not so wide as to interfere with movement

FORELEGS parallel, straight, strongly boned, muscular set close to body under shoulder blades

COLOR: Any solid color other than black, and any such color with tan points; shade to be uniform, but lighter feathering permissible. (See COLOR, Black variety, re requirements of tan points.)

SKULL somewhat rounded, no tendency toward flatness; bony structure beneath eyes well-chiseled

BODY short, compact; distance from top of shoulders to ground 15% more than from same point to set-on of tail

EARS lobular, placed on line no higher than lower part of eye; leather long, fine

NECK long enough to allow nose to reach ground easily; muscular; not throaty; slight arch

BACK strong, sloping evenly and slightly downward from shoulders to set-on of tail

TAIL docked; set on line with topline or slightly higher

COAT on head, short, fine; on body, silky, flat or slightly wavy; ears, chest, abdomen and legs well but not excessively feathered

HIPS wide; quarters well-rounded; muscular

HIND LEGS parallel; strongly-boned; muscular

HOCKS strong, well-let-down, parallel in motion or at rest

HEIGHT: Ideally, 15" for adult dogs 14" for adult bitches

RIBS deep, well-sprung

PASTERNS short, strong

FEET compact, round, firm, turning neither in nor out; pads thick, strong, horny

DISQUALIFICATIONS: Males over 15½" height; Females, 14½". Tan markings in excess of 10%. White markings except on chest and throat. Absence of tan markings in each of specified locations. (See COLOR, Black variety.)

Visualization of the Breed Standard for ASCOB COCKER SPANIELS
(Reproduced with permission from DOG STANDARDS ILLUSTRATED © 1975 Howell Book House Inc.)

Eyes—Eyeballs are round and full and look directly forward. The shape of the eye rims gives a slightly almond-shaped appearance; the eye is not weak or goggled. The color of the iris is dark brown and in general the darker the better. The expression is intelligent, alert, soft and appealing.

Ears—Lobular, long, of fine leather, well feathered, and placed no higher than a line to the lower part of the eye.

Neck and Shoulders—The neck is sufficiently long to allow the nose to reach the ground easily, muscular and free from pendulous "throatiness." It rises strongly from the shoulders and arches slightly as it tapers to join the head. The shoulders are well laid back forming an angle with the upper arm of approximately 90 degrees which permits the dog to move his forelegs in an easy manner with considerable forward reach. Shoulders are clean-cut and sloping without protrusion and so set that the upper points of the withers are at an angle which permits a wide spring of rib.

Body—The body is short, compact and firmly knit together, giving an impression of strength. The distance from the highest point of the shoulder blades to the ground is fifteen (15%) percent or approximately two inches more than the length from this point to the set-on of the tail. Back is strong and sloping evenly and slightly downward from the shoulders to the set-on of the docked tail. Hips are wide and quarters well rounded and muscular. The chest is deep, its lowest point no higher than the elbows, its front sufficiently wide for adequate heart and lung space, yet not so wide as to interfere with the straightforward movement of the forelegs. Ribs are deep and well sprung. The Cocker Spaniel never appears long and low.

Tail—The docked tail is set on and carried on a line with the topline of the back, or slightly higher; never straight up like a terrier and never so low as to indicate timidity. When the dog is in motion the tail action is merry.

Legs and Feet—Forelegs are parallel, straight, strongly boned and muscular and set close to the body well under the scapulae. When viewed from the side with the forelegs vertical, the elbow is directly below the highest point of the shoulder blade. The pasterns are short and strong. The hind legs are strongly boned and muscled with good

187

GENERAL APPEARANCE: Sturdy, compact, completely balanced. Sound. Even-tempered, free, merry.

COAT on head—short, fine; on body—silky, flat or slightly wavy; ears, chest, abdomen and legs well but not excessively feathered

SKULL somewhat rounded, no tendency toward flatness; bony structure beneath eyes well-chiseled

EYES slightly almond-shaped appearance; eyeballs round, full; iris dark brown

STOP pronounced, eyebrows clearly defined

NOSE size to balance muzzle and foreface; may be brown, liver or black, darker the better; well-developed nostrils

CHEEKS smooth, clean cut;

TEETH sound, not too small, scissors bite

MUZZLE broad, deep; distance from tip of nose to stop is half that from stop to base of skull; jaws square, even; upper lip should cover lower jaw

CHEST deep, lowest point no higher than elbows; not so wide as to interfere with movement

FORELEGS parallel, straight, strongly boned, muscular; set close to body under shoulder blades

BODY short, compact; distance from tip of shoulders to ground 15% more than from same point to set-on of tail

EARS lobular, placed on line no higher than lower part of eye; leather long, fine

NECK long enough to allow nose to reach ground easily; muscular; not throaty; slight arch

SHOULDERS well laid back; clean-cut sloping without protrusion

BACK strong, sloping evenly and slightly downward from shoulders to set-on of tail

TAIL docked, set on line with topline or slightly higher

HIPS wide; quarters well-rounded; muscular

HIND LEGS parallel; strongly-boned; muscular

STIFLES well-angulated

HOCKS strong, well-let-down, parallel in motion or at rest

FEET compact, round, firm; turning neither in nor out; pads thick, strong, horny

RIBS deep, well-sprung

PASTERNS short, strong

HEIGHT: Ideally, 15″ for adult dogs 14″ for adult bitches

COLOR: Two or more definite, well-broken colors, one of which must be white, including those with tan points. Roans classified as Parti-colors.

DISQUALIFICATIONS: 90% or more of primary color. Tan markings in excess of 10%. Males over 15½″ in height; bitches over 14½″.

Visualization of the Breed Standard for PARTI-COLOR COCKER SPANIELS
(Reproduced with permission from DOG STANDARDS ILLUSTRATED © 1978 Howell Book House Inc.)

angulation at the stifle and powerful, clearly defined thighs. The stifle joint is strong and there is no slippage of it in motion or when standing. The hocks are strong, well let down, and when viewed from behind, the hind legs are parallel when in motion and at rest.

Feet—Compact, large, round and firm with horny pads; they turn neither in nor out. Dewclaws on hind legs and forelegs may be removed.

Coat—On the head, short and fine; on the body, medium length, with enough undercoating to give protection. The ears, chest, abdomen and legs are well feathered, but not so excessively as to hide the Cocker Spaniel's true lines and movement or affect his appearance and function as a sporting dog. The *texture* is most important. The coat is silky, flat or slightly wavy, and of a texture which permits easy care. Excessive or curly or cottony textured coat is to be penalized.

Color and Markings —

Black Variety—Solid color black, to include black with tan points. The black should be jet; shadings of brown or liver in the sheen of the coat is not desirable. A small amount of white on the chest and/or throat is allowed, white in any other location shall disqualify.

Any Solid Color Other Than Black Variety — Any solid color other than black and any such color with tan points. The color shall be of a uniform shade, but lighter coloring of the feather is permissible. A small amount of white on the chest and/or throat is allowed, white in any other location shall disqualify.

Parti-Color Variety—Two or more definite, well-broken colors, one of which must be white, including those with tan points; it is preferable that the tan markings be located in the same pattern as for the tan points in the Black and ASCOB varieties. Roans are classified as parti-colors, and may be of any of the usual roaning patterns. Primary color which is ninety percent (90%) or more shall disqualify.

Tan Points—The color of the tan may be from the lightest cream to the darkest red color and should be restricted to ten percent (10%) or less of the color of the specimen, tan markings in excess of that amount shall disqualify.

In the case of tan points in the Black or ASCOB varieties, the markings shall be located as follows:

(1) A clear tan spot over each eye.
(2) On the sides of the muzzle and on the cheeks.

Cocker outline in the 1940s. This painting of Ch. Biggs' Cover Charge, a notable red sire whelped in 1944, hangs in the offices of the American Kennel Club in New York City. Cover Charge was bred and owned by Robert W. Biggs.

(3) On the undersides of the ears.
(4) On all feet and/or legs.
(5) Under the tail.
(6) On the chest, optional, presence or absence not penalized.

Tan markings which are not readily visible or which amount only to traces, shall be penalized. Tan on the muzzle which extends upward, over and joins shall also be penalized. The absence of tan markings in the Black or ASCOB variety in each of the specified locations in an otherwise tan-pointed dog shall disqualify.

Movement—The Cocker Spaniel, though the smallest of the sporting dogs, possesses a typical sporting dog gait. Prerequisite to good movement is balance between the front and rear assemblies. He drives with his strong, powerful rear quarters and is properly constructed in the shoulders and forelegs so that he can reach forward without constriction in a full stride to counterbalance the driving force from the rear. Above all, his gait is co-ordinated, smooth and effortless. The dog must cover ground with his action and excessive animation should never be mistaken for proper gait.

Height—The ideal height at the withers for an adult dog is 15 inches and for an adult bitch 14 inches. Height may vary one-half inch above or below this ideal. A dog whose height exceeds $15\frac{1}{2}$ inches or a bitch whose height exceeds $14\frac{1}{4}$ inches shall be disqualified. An adult dog whose height is less than $14\frac{1}{2}$ inches or an adult bitch whose height is less than $13\frac{1}{2}$ inches shall be penalized.

Note: Height is determined by a line perpendicular to the ground from the top of the shoulder blades, the dog standing naturally with its forelegs and the lower hind legs parallel to the line of measurement.

DISQUALIFICATIONS:

Color and Markings Disqualifications:
In *Black* and *Any Solid Color Other Than Black* varieties:
White markings except on the chest and/or throat.
In dogs with tan points—the absence of tan markings in each of the specified locations.
Tan markings in excess of ten percent (10%).
In *Parti-Color* variety:
Ninety percent (90%) or more of primary color.

Height Disqualifications:
Males over 15½ inches; females over 14½ inches.

— Approved June 9, 1981
— Effective January 1, 1982

ANATOMY OF THE COCKER SPANIEL

Drawings by ROBERT F. WAY, V.M.D., M.S.

(Reproduced with permission from DOG STANDARDS ILLUSTRATED, formerly published as Visualizations of the Dog Standards © 1975 Howell Book House Inc.)

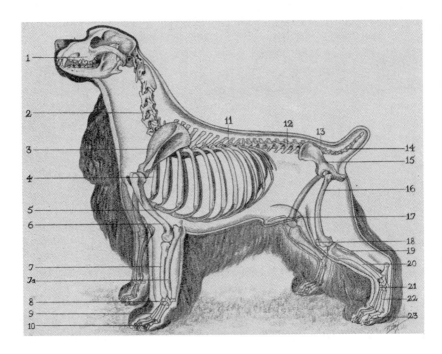

The Skeleton

1 Skull	9 Metacarpal Bones	17 Os Penis
2 Seven Cervical Vertebrae	10 Phalangeal Bones	18 Patella
3 Scapula	11 Thoracic Vertebrae—Thirteen	19 Fibula
4 Ribs—Thirteen Pairs	12 Lumbar Vertebrae—Seven	20 Tibia
5 Sternum	13 Sacrum	21 Tarsal Bones
6 Humerus	14 Coccygeal Vertebrae	22 Metatarsal B
7 Radius; 7a Ulna	15 Os Coxae	23 Phalangeal
8 Carpal Bones	16 Femur	

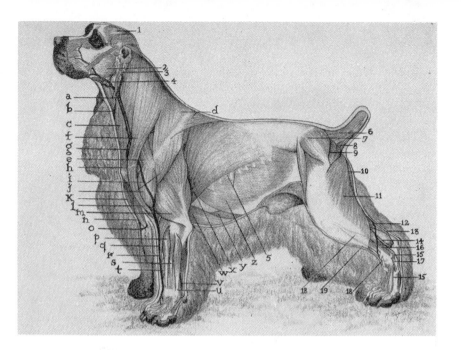

Superficial Structures

a External Jugular Vein
b Sternohyoideus Muscle
c Sternomastoideus Muscle
d Trapezius Muscle
e Omotransversarius Muscle
f Clavicular Head of Trapezius
g Cleido-mastoideus Muscle
h Rudimentary Clavicle
i Branch of Cephalic Vein
j Deltoideus Muscle
k Pectoralis Major Muscle
l Clavicular Head of Deltoideus
m Triceps Brachii Muscle
n Biceps Brachii Muscle
o Median Cubital Vein

p Common Digital Extensor Muscle
q Cephalic Vein
r Extensor Carpi Radialis Muscle
s Lateral Digital Extensor Muscle
t Abductor Pollicis Longus Muscle
u Extensor Carpi Ulnaris Muscle
v Flexor Carpi Ulnaris Muscle
w Back Portion of Pectoralis Major
x Latissimus Dorsi Muscle
y Rectus Abdominis Muscle
z External Oblique Abdominal Muscle
1 Temperal Muscle
2 Masseter Muscle
3 Parotid Salivary Gland
4 Mandibular Salivary Gland

The Bones

5 External Intercostal Muscles
6 Dorsal Sacrococcygeus Muscle
7 Gluteus Medius Muscle
8 Coccygeus Muscle
9 Gluteus Maximus Muscle
10 Semitendinosus Muscle
11 Biceps Femoris Muscle
12 Small Saphenous Vein

13 Calcanean Tendon
14 Flexor Hallucis Longus Muscle
15 Peroneus Digiti Quinti Muscle
16 Peroneus Brevis Muscle
17 Peroneus Longus Muscle
18 Long Digital Extensor Muscle
19 Anterior Tibial Muscle

193

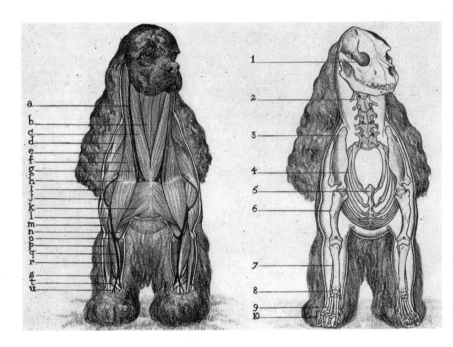

Superficial Structures

a External Jugular Vein
b Sternohyoideus Muscle
c Sternomastoideus Muscle
d Trapezius Muscle
e Omotransversarius Muscle
f Clavicular Head of Trapezius
g Cleido-mastoideus Muscle
h Rudimentary Clavicle
i Branch of Cephalic Vein
j Deltoideus Muscle
k Pectoralis Maior Muscle

l Clavicular Head of Deltoideus
m Triceps Brachii Muscle
n Biceps Brachii Muscle
o Median Cubital Vein
p Common Digital Extensor Muscle
q Cephalic Vein
r Extensor Carpi Radialis Muscle
s Lateral Digital Extensor Muscle
t Abductor Pollicis Longus Muscle
u Accessory Cephalic Vein

The Bones

1 Skull

2 Cervical Vertebrae

3 Scapula

4 Ribs

5 Sternum

6 Humerus

7 Radius and Ulna

8 Carpal Bones

9 Metacarpal Bones

10 Phalangeal Bones

194

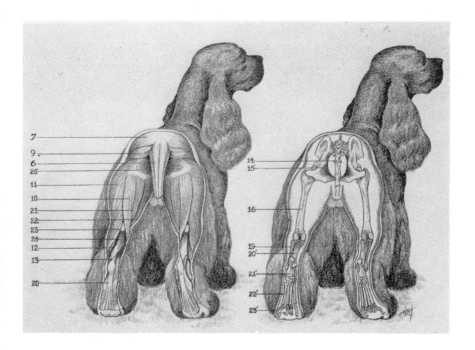

Superficial Structures

7 Gluteus Medius Muscle
9 Gluteus Maximus Muscle
6 Dorsal Sacroccygeus Muscle
25 Obturator Internus Muscle
11 Biceps Femoris Muscle
10 Semitendinosus Muscle
21 Semimembranosus Muscle

22 Gracilis Muscle
23 Popliteal Lymph Gland
24 Gastrocnemius Muscle
12 Small Saphenous Vein
13 Calcanean Tendon
20 Superficial Digital Flexor Tendon

The Bones

14 Coccygeal Vertebrae
15 Os Coxae
16 Femur
19 Fibula

20' Tibia
21' Tarsal Bones
22' Metatarsal Bones
23' Phalangeal Bones

195

Too snipy. Muzzle does not balance.

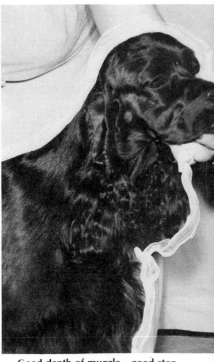

Good depth of muzzle—good stop.

Too deep in muzzle—coarse head.

196

9

The Standard
Examined in Depth

Except for the section on Color and Markings, which was newly revised effective January 1982, the current Cocker Spaniel standard dates from February 1, 1973.

The 1973 Standard was the result of several years of study and hard work by a Standards Committee of which I was chairman. Six revisions were submitted to the membership. Whenever there was sufficient dissatisfaction with any particular point, or where requests had been made for additional clarification, the wishes of the members were given precedence over those of the Committee members.

It had been 16 years since the previous Standard. While there were many "good things" to be retained, many changes were called for to bring the Standard up-to-date so that it described *today's* Cocker, which has again caught the Fancy's eye throughout the nation.

The paragraph of description appears now at the beginning of the Standard rather than at the end as before. This is where it belongs.

The Standard no longer has a scale of points. The elimination of this scale was at the suggestion of the American Kennel Club. It is their feeling that such a scale is confusing to judges rather than helpful, as there is a tendency to check only the scale rather than the details of the Standard.

Following General Appearance, the Standard describes the correct head and all its parts. While this description is very clear, still there are many totally different heads that will still meet the Standard. This can be brought about by exaggeration in the various parts. To have a number of successful breeders reach complete agreement on what constitutes a perfectly proportioned head would be almost impossible. But, as we all know, many heads can, in the owner's eyes, meet these dimensions properly and still one can see a difference in each and every one.

The Standard calls for a **skull** rounded, but not exaggerated, with no tendency toward flatness. The latter is rarely seen today. The eyebrows are clearly defined with a pronounced stop. This is one place where I feel there is not great uniformity. The blacks and black and tans seem to meet the Standard closer than the other two colors, although I have seen improvement in the buffs and partis during the past few years.

The paragraph describing **the muzzle** is very clear and needs little or no elaboration. Probably the greatest variation in muzzles seen today is in the depth and breadth. Balance is most important and if the muzzle is a bit refined, but balances with the skull, it should be acceptable. One will also find very often where the length of the nose seems long but if it still meets the Standard requirement of being half the length of the crown, it must be accepted.

The paragraph on **teeth** is a short one and simply calls for a scissors bite. This means that when the mouth is shut, the inside of the front upper teeth are over the outside edge of the lower teeth, meeting tightly in this position. Many judges will accept an even bite—this is where the judges will differ in opinion. There is also a tendency in recent years to find exceptionally large eye teeth. In some cases, they will not permit the mouth to close completely. This can cause a wry mouth that is ugly and most certainly a fault. It is my belief that this is an inherent factor and should be watched closely in breeding.

The next paragraph is on the **nose.** This should be of sufficient size to balance the muzzle and foreface, with well developed nostrils typical of a sporting dog, the blacker the better. Brown or liver is allowed in chocolates and in some other colors, but is not as attractive as the black. Above all, the color of the nose must harmonize with the color of the eye rim.

The color of the nose can vary sometimes during the year due to the climate. This is often called a "weather nose," as it gets lighter in the winter and darkens in the summer.

HEADS – full view.

Muzzle not full enough.
Indistinct stop. High ear set.

Correct proportion of head.

Skully; overdone. Droopy eyes.

199

Eyes—This paragraph is very clear and if studied, certainly gives a clear picture of what is desired. Beautiful eyes are the heritage of the Cocker Spaniel. Goggle eyes are not desired but a large, expressive, appealing eye is one reason for the Cocker's popularity.

The paragraph on **Ears** is a short one and to the point. The long ears have been a distinctive part of the Cocker Spaniel through the years. The ideal ear is long and pendulant and is joined to the head in a fold. This permits the ear to fit close to the head. The placement is most important—*"not higher than a line to the lower part of the eye."*

The next paragraph, in my opinion, is one of the most important in the description of what is desired in the Cocker Spaniel. **Correct neck and shoulders** are a joy to see. First of all, the neck must be sufficiently long to allow the nose to reach the ground easily, muscular and free from pendulous throatiness. This calls for a muscular neck but still it should have a clean, lean appearance, and with proper length it will have this look. *"The neck rises strongly from the shoulders and arches slightly as it tapers to join the head."*

The neck and shoulders are an assembly that must fit together for perfection. *"The shoulders are well laid back forming an angle with the upper arm of approximately 90 degrees, which permits the dog to move his forelegs in an easy manner with considerable forward reach."* It is difficult to discuss neck and shoulders separately as the angulation of shoulder blade (scapula) in the shoulder construction governs the length of neck.

While the neck is the link between the head and the body, it must be strong enough for that purpose. With the higher stationed dog of today, the neck has necessarily grown longer. However, too long a neck is seldom seen; more often we see one too short. An arched neck denotes strength and enables the head to be carried in a straightforward position rather than sloping upward.

A neck with a concave topline is called an "ewe neck," which is undesirable. It denotes weakness and usually insufficient strength to properly support the head.

The width of the neck should gradually increase until it fits smoothly into well laid back shoulders upon which it must depend. The more nearly the juncture of the shoulder blade (scapula) approximates a right angle with the bone (humerus) of the upper arm, the better the shoulder and the greater the support of the neck.

Shoulders should be checked from two positions. They should be observed from the side and from behind and above the dog. Shoulders

Short neck. Front legs too far forward.

Proper layback; front well placed.

Set too far under. Short neck.

Topline too level.

Proper slope. Good layback.

Poor topline. Drop back of withers and before tailset.

which are too straight up and down (steep) do not allow the proper length of neck. This can be seen from a side view. When viewed from above and behind the dog, one must feel as well as look. Locate the tips of the shoulder blades at the withers. The tips of the blades should not be too close together nor too wide apart. The width here is most important. If too wide, you will not have a smooth shoulder and you will lack the desired lay-back. If too close, you will not have free movement and the gait will probably be spraddled. The space between the blades will differ in different size dogs, but I would say the ideal in a normal size dog would be about 1½ inches.

Body—*"The body is short, compact and firmly knit together, giving an impression of strength."* This paragraph or sentence covers a lot of ground but still in one's mind, gives the picture of a short, cobby little dog that well deserves his place in the Sporting Group.

"The distance from the highest point of the shoulder blades to the ground is fifteen (15%) per cent or approximately two inches more than the length from this point to the set-on of the tail." This was an excellent addition to the new Standard as the Cocker has definitely come up on leg considerably during the past decade, and the previous Standard did not come close to describing the Cocker of today.

"Back is strong and sloping evenly and slightly downward from the shoulders to the set-on of the docked tail." This gives us an excellent description of the topline desired on today's Cocker.

"Hips are wide and quarters well rounded and muscular. The chest is deep, its lowest point no higher than the elbows, its front sufficiently wide for adequate heart and lung space, yet not so wide as to interfere with the straightforward movement of the forelegs. Ribs are deep and well sprung." This paragraph gives an adequate description of the body, and should be clearly understood by all who read it.

"The Cocker Spaniel never appears long and low." A positive and decisive statement that should be adhered to in breeding.

Tail—This is a very important part of the Standard and is often ignored. *"The docked tail is set on and carried on a line with the topline of the back, or slightly higher; never straight up like a terrier and never so low as to indicate timidity. When the dog is in motion the tail action is merry."*

This paragraph was a complete change from the previous one. At no place in the old Standard was it mentioned that the tail of the Cocker was docked. This was called to the attention of the Committee by the

Coat texture too wooly.

Proper coat.

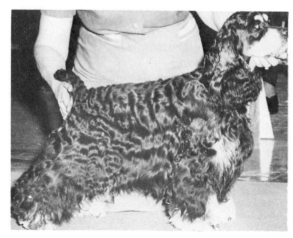

Coat too curly.

AKC. The carriage of the tail is emphasized and unfortunately too little attention is paid to this as many terrier tails are seen in the ring today.

The next paragraph in the Standard is on **"Legs and Feet."** *"Forelegs are parallel, straight, strongly boned and muscular and set close to the body well under the scapulae. When viewed from the side with the forelegs vertical, the elbow is directly below the highest point of the shoulder blade. The pasterns are short and strong."* The forelegs should be absolutely straight with exception that at the pastern joint a very slight bend is permitted. This allows a certain amount of give when the dog is moving. There should, however, be no weakness at the pasterns as this is a fault.

"The hind legs are strongly boned and muscled with good angulation at the stifle and powerful clearly defined thighs. The stifle joint is strong and there is no slippage of it in motion or when standing."

"The hocks are strong, well let down, and when viewed from behind, the hind legs are parallel when in motion and at rest."

While this paragraph is quite clear, emphasis should be placed on the low hock, close to the ground, which, together with a stifle joint that is well bent and long, enables the dog to drive and cover much ground.

Feet—*"Compact, large, round and firm with horny pads; they turn neither in nor out. Dewclaws on hind legs and forelegs may be removed."* The mention of dewclaws is required by the AKC.

The next paragraph is on **"Coat."** This is a lengthy paragraph and describes in detail the coat emphasizing the texture. It also calls attention to excessive coat which should not be so great as *"to hide the Cocker Spaniel's true lines and movement or affect his appearance and function as a sporting dog."*

The texture that is called for is one that is silky, flat or slightly wavy, and of a texture which permits easy care. Excessive or curly or cottony coat is to be penalized. There is no doubt that this paragraph is being observed as fewer such coats are being seen today.

The next paragraph on **Color and Markings** is very important. The black variety must be jet black with no shading of brown or liver in the coat. A small amount of white on the chest and throat is allowed but must be penalized, but white in any other location is disqualified.

The Black variety, at one time, was the dominant variety and very few ASCOBs or parti-colors reached prominence in the Groups. This condition has changed greatly during the past decade as the improvement in the Parti-colors and the ASCOBS has been so great.

One of the important changes effected in the January 1982 revision of the Standard is that the Black and Tan, formerly included with the ASCOB variety for show purposes, is now included with the Black variety.

The new color section continues the provision that the Any Solid Color Other Than Black variety (buffs and reds) may include those with lighter feathering. Coloring under this heading may vary from the very light cream (often called silver) to the very dark reds. The penalty for white on the chest is the same as for the Blacks.

The 1982 revision clearly spells out the requirements covering the tan points in the Black or ASCOB varieties. It again specifies that the markings should be located as follows:

(1) A clear tan spot over each eye.
(2) On the sides of the muzzle and on the cheeks.
(3) On the undersides of the ears.
(4) On all feet and/or legs.
(5) Under the tail.

The absence of tan markings in these locations in an otherwise tan-pointed dog of the Black or ASCOB varieties shall disqualify. Tan on the muzzle, which extends upward, over and joins shall be penalized. However, tan markings on the chest is optional, and presence or absence is not to be penalized.

Another important 1982 change specifies that tan markings which are not readily visible (or which amount only to traces), which in the 1973 Standard had called for disqualification, are now to be penalized.

The new Parti-Color stipulation reads: Two or more definite, *well-broken* colors, one of which must be white, including those with tan points; it is preferable that the tan markings be located in the same pattern as for the tan points in the Black and ASCOB varieties.

Primary color which is 90% or more shall disqualify.

Roans are classified as Parti-colors, and may be of any of the usual roaning patterns.

Movement—*"The Cocker Spaniel, though the smallest of the sporting dogs, possesses a typical sporting dog gait."* After all the details of structure have been evaluated, it becomes necessary to see the dog in

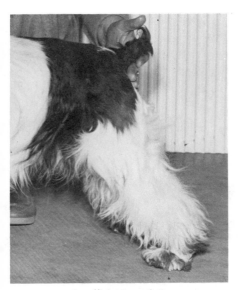

Insufficient angulation.

Correct bend of stifle.
Well let down hocks.

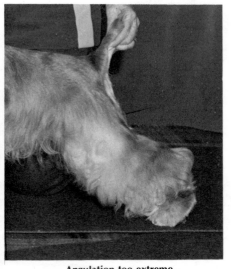

Angulation too extreme.

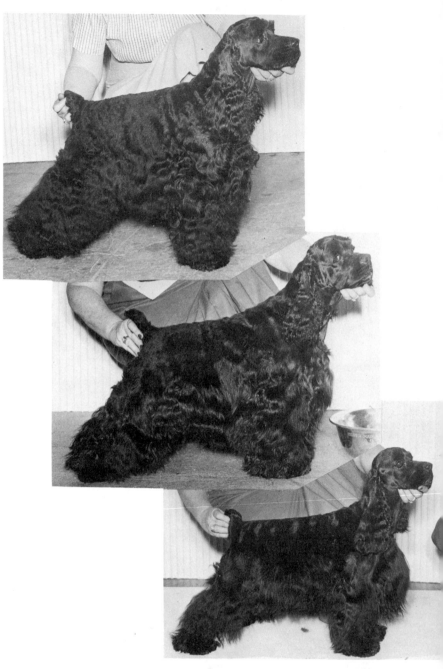

BALANCE. Top: **Incorrect balance; too short-coupled,** Center: **Good proportion – height, length of body and neck.** Below: **Too long in back for height; straight shoulder.**

208

action. No matter how excellent in conformation, he must be able to move correctly. *"Prerequisite to good movement is balance between the front and rear assemblies. He drives with his strong, powerful rear quarters and is properly constructed in the shoulders and forelegs so that he can reach forward without constriction in a full stride to counterbalance the driving force from the rear."* This indicates that the entire power of movement in the dog is generated in the hindquarters, the bones acting as levers moved by powerful muscles.

"Above all, his gait is coordinated, smooth and effortless. The dog must cover ground with his action and excessive animation should never be mistaken for proper gait."

Very often one sees a dog shown with such speed that it is impossible to properly evaluate the gait. Unfortunately, some judges seem to think this excessive speed is desirable.

Note that a detailed discussion of Cocker movement, and the factors that influence it, will be found at the end of Chapter 12 of this book (How to Show the Cocker Spaniel.)

Height—*"The ideal height at the withers for an adult dog is 15 inches and for an adult bitch is 14 inches. Height may vary one-half an inch. A dog whose height exceeds 15½ inches or a bitch whose height exceeds 14½ inches shall be disqualified."*

The important change in this paragraph from our previous Standard is the penalty for minimum height. *"An adult dog whose height is less than 14½ inches or an adult bitch whose height is less than 13½ inches shall be penalized."*

Height is determined by a line perpendicular to the ground from the top of the shoulderblades, the dog standing naturally with the forelegs and the lower hind legs parallel to the line of measurement.

There has been great concern among breeders about the small dogs and bitches being shown and winning. The Standard Committee spent a great deal of time considering this matter and unanimously came to the conclusion that a penalty was in order.

Disqualifications are listed in detail in the Standard. There is no change from the old Standard on disqualifications except on the Black and Tans. Reasons for this disqualification are outlined under the heading "Black and Tans" in this article.

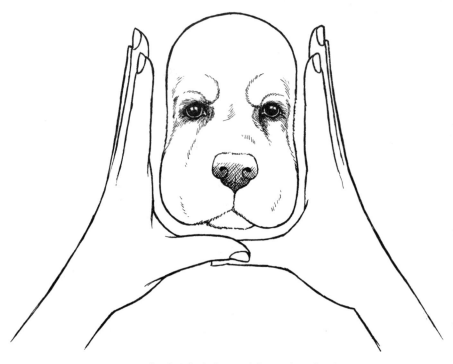

Evaluating the balance of the Cocker's head.

10

Choosing a
Cocker Spaniel Puppy

THERE are many things to consider when you get ready to buy a puppy. So often buyers will purchase on impulse when they see a cute puppy in the window of a pet shop. Whether you are seeking a puppy for the show ring, obedience work or a well-bred pet, you will want one that is healthy, full of pep, with a lustrous coat, bright, clear eyes, four good legs and a wagging tail.

Most conscientious breeders like to wait until the puppies are nine weeks old before letting them go to a new owner. This gives time for permanent vaccine inoculation for distemper, hepatitis and leptospirosis. This means added protection for the new owner and the breeder.

If you are purchasing your puppy from a breeder, you should be able to learn a great deal more about the background of the litter than if purchased from a commercial shop where they just buy and sell.

Most dedicated breeders are glad to go into detail as to the special care they have given their puppies. In most cases, they have made preparation for this event long before it happened. They will have seen that their bitch was in top condition physically, and that she was free of internal and external parasites. They will have fortified her with Vitamin D and calcium for several weeks before she whelped.

This could prevent a convulsion caused by lack of calcium in the system. This can prove very serious if veterinarian's help is not secured.

Occasionally, in a very young litter just starting to walk, a breeder will have what is termed a "swimmer." This is usually a fat, heavy puppy whose legs seem too weak to hold him up. In most cases, with help, this puppy will recover and be a normal healthy pup. He should be given rough material on which to try and walk. A few times each day, he should be placed in a swing with his feet off the floor so he can work his legs. This will help to strengthen his legs and straighten them. They will usually recover very quickly this way. If allowed to go on without help he may mature into a misshapen puppy whose legs seem to come out of the four corners.

If the mother has a good supply of milk, this will do much to give the pups a good start during the first three weeks. If she is lacking in milk this is where the experienced breeder will pitch in and supplement with a preparation called "Esbilac" which is very similar to the mother's milk. Constant, steady growth is necessary for the building of strong bone structure in the puppy.

When the pups are three weeks of age, the experienced breeder will start feeding. The pups will usually start lapping the Esbilac out of the pan at that time. Then, start adding a little of the mother's food which the puppies usually relish. By increasing the amount each day, by the time the litter is six weeks old they can be completely weaned from the mother.

Do not ever keep a timid pup for your show puppy. In some cases, he can be brought out of this timidity by a lot of individual attention. If he is good enough in conformation, he should be placed in a show home where he will get a lot of attention and be made to feel important.

In evaluating the six weeks old puppy, I look at the head first. The stop (that indentation between the eyes) should be deep at this age. The eyes should be dark and look straight forward and be cleanly chiseled beneath. This means the structure under the eyes should be smooth with no bumps or fullness.

In checking the skull and muzzle, I like to place my forefingers on each side of the skull. Then, with my thumbs across the muzzle, I form a rectangle. If this rectangle is the same distance across the muzzle as it is across the skull, the puppy will have a properly proportioned head. One rarely finds the front of the muzzle wider than the skull. You are more apt to find the reverse—a skull too wide for the muzzle. The head usually grows in proportion to the rate of the all over growth and, at maturity, the skull would probably be too wide for the foreface.

The ears on this two months old puppy should be placed not higher

Cocker Spaniel puppies – 8 weeks old.

Just past 3 months of age. Moody's Tri to Remember and Moody's Certain Smile, bred and owned by Paul and Jane Moody.

213

than a line to the corner of the eye, as stated clearly in the Standard. Above all, they should hang in a lobular fashion, not flat as we see occasionally.

Front legs should be straight and set well under the body. The rear legs should be well angulated, and if they have a tendency to be wobbly or hock in a bit at this age, it is not alarming as maturity will improve this condition. Coupling should be fairly short but still with enough length to allow free movement of the hocks. The layback of shoulders, ribspring, depth of brisket, muscling of rear legs and coat factor can come with maturity.

Just one bad fault can move the show puppy into the pet classification. At two months of age, it is difficult to completely eliminate some puppies. They can have many good things and just one or two questionable faults. There may be a slight overbite or perhaps the complete lack of brisket which might throw you off in your evaluation, as puppies this age rarely have much brisket.

If you find an exceptionally good head and good bone structure on a two months old puppy, it is worth taking a chance on keeping for the present. Shoulder placement can change a lot, so it is foolish to eliminate a puppy because of shoulders that are too erect at this young age.

The pet puppy should have good temperament and this is something that should be watched carefully in breeding. It has been our policy for forty years to never breed either sex if they show any tendency toward extreme shyness or bad temper. We believe that temperament can be controlled just as well as other traits.

We go now to the four months old show prospect. At this age, it is well to ignore certain things. The lack of stop should not be of great concern, as this is the age when the deep stop is starting to smooth out and become plain. If height at the shoulder is a concern, there is still time for the puppy to come up on leg. The coat may not be everything you want, but there is still time for it to grow. Now is the time to be sure your puppy has the right temperament for a show dog—with a tail that always wags.

The four months old pet puppy should have been sold by now if the faults you saw at two months of age have not improved. Do not make the mistake of keeping a questionable puppy too long. Your wishful thinking does not always pan out. Too, you will become attached to him and completely overlook his faults even though you are aware of them.

If you have decided definitely by now that your pet puppy is just that and you do not want to keep him, now is the time to make every effort

3 months old. Puppy who later became Ch. High Sky Harlequin, pictured with his sire Ch. Silver Maple Sharp Tri-Umph.

Ch. Sagamore Golden Rhythm as a 4-months old puppy. Owned by Nancy Block.

215

to place him in a good home where he will be loved and cared for. You must remember that you have a purebred dog and while he may not measure up to the show dog, he is still a beautiful Cocker and will make someone a lovely pet. Do not price him too low as people sometimes look down on the puppy they have purchased cheaply. It is never good to downgrade any of your dogs. Be honest and tell the new owner that while he is not a top show dog, he is beautiful and will make a wonderful pet and one they can be proud of owning.

You do not want this Cocker, just because you have placed him in the pet class, to be criticized by the new owner. You want him to have a good home for the balance of his life. The average person wanting a good pet will understand.

The next consideration is the six months old puppy. This is the time to look for height at the shoulder. This is different in the various bloodlines. Pups from some bloodlines seem to get their height sooner than others and then stop growing when six or seven months of age. Others will continue to grow and may add as much as an inch after reaching six months of age. If you have purchased your pup from a breeder, this is something to question him about. He should know from experience if he has sold you a fast growing pup or one that is slow in maturing.

The coat at six months of age should be coming in fast. Watch the front of the legs for good growth there. If the front of the legs is still slick and smooth, there is a chance you may never have a profuse coat.

The head may still be at a plain stage. The Cocker head grows in length until about seven months of age when it starts broadening and it is this process that brings back the stop.

Watch your pup at this age closely for the development of the rib cage and brisket, also the muscling of the hocks and the topline when moving.

At six months of age, if you find anything about your show puppy that might keep it from being a winner, unless it is a bitch and you want to keep her for breeding because of her bloodlines, I would try and find a good home for it. If it is a male, I would try even harder to place him at this time.

At nine months of age, you should be very sure whether you have a show dog or not. If he has failed you in any respect, it should show up by now. If he has not, then you have only to wait for full maturity as far as coat and normal development.

If it is a show dog you are wanting, check the following things at this

216

Moody's Movin' On at 5 months of age.

Moody's Movin' On at 8 months of age.

217

4 months old. Dreamridge Double Date became the dam of 5 champions. Bred and owned by Tom O'Neal.

Ch. Dreamridge Dr. Pepper at 5 months of age.

218

time. His stop has returned, giving his head a very pleasing appearance. He should have the layback of shoulders that is necessary for length of neck. His brisket and rib cage should be developing. His front legs should be set well under his body and his elbows should fit tightly against him. His rear legs should be well angulated and the hocks should come straight back. His topline should slope slightly toward the rear with his merry tail coming straight off the back.

You may still have to wait for some maturity—more coat, a little more spring of rib, but if the dog has the right frame, time will give that finished look you desire.

Always keep in mind that every good puppy does not become a champion, but every champion was a good puppy.

One of the Dreamridge puppies has reached maturity.

The completed dog with correct outline.

11

Grooming the Cocker for Show

Drawings by Peggy Bang

THIS chapter will be devoted primarily to the trimming of the *show* Cocker. In the chapter on Care and Training you will find a brief description of how to trim a pet Cocker. However, those desiring to have their pet look like a show dog should follow directions given in this chapter.

If you examine closely the pictures of top show winners, it will help you visualize the pattern you are trying to follow. Also, read the Standard of the breed so you will know the faults and disqualifications you must avoid.

You will need the following equipment: An Oster Clipper with #10 and #15 blades; a pair of sharp straight shears and two pairs of thinning shears, regular and fine. I prefer the thinning shears with the teeth on one side only. You will need a blow dryer. A stand dryer is best but a hand dryer can be used. A steady table is also needed.

The work of preparing the Cocker for the show ring should be divided into three parts. First, rough in the work that can be handled with the clippers. Next, bathe and dry the dog using the blow dryer. The final stage is the scissoring work which is the most difficult and requires much practice.

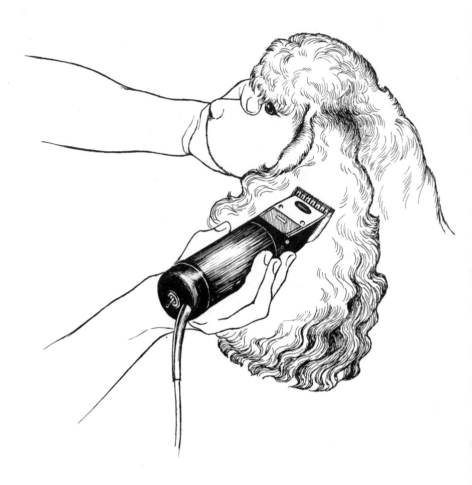

The roughing in work that must be done with the clippers is on the
head, neck and shoulders. With the #10 blade, trim the outer and inner
sides of the ear, going against the grain. Begin the first stroke upward
on the outside of the ear, about one-third of the way down from where
the ear joins the head. At the back edge of the ear, this distance is
slightly less so this line conforms to the shape of the ear. When the top
of the ear is reached, as you finish your stroke, roll your clipper slightly
upward to avoid sharp lines.

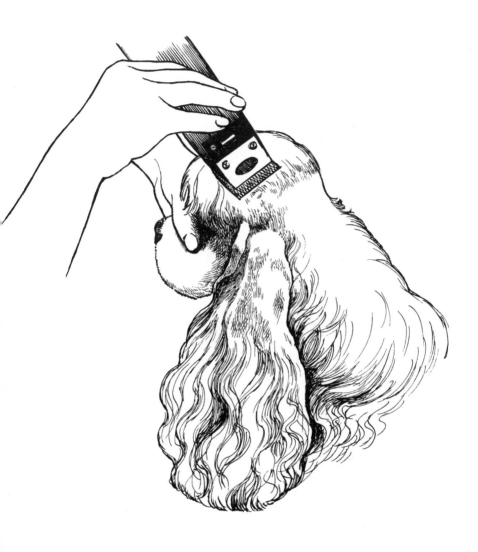

Another place to use the clipper is for a strip across the back skull about ½ inch wide, from ear to ear, over the occiput. This will give a clean look in this area. Be careful not to start too far back as this will affect the arch of the neck.

Next, go to the front and start with your clippers just above the breastbone and clean the underside of the neck and the lower jaw. Either a #10 or a #15 can be used for this area depending upon the thickness of the hair. Trim close to the area with folds in the lower jaw where the hair is apt to hold saliva. Trim the balance of the neck, excepting that part between the ears, with the #10 clipper and go with the hair. Trim downward from the base of the ear and from the part just finished to a line just back of the ear. Do not go quite to the shoulder muscle. This part should be done with the scissors as well as the finishing of the top of the neck.

Returning to the head, the area between the ear and the corner of the mouth can be trimmed against the grain. Be careful not to go beyond the corner of the mouth, nor above the corner of the eye on the line to the ear. The sides and back, as well as the shoulders and withers should all be done with the thinning shears. None of this part should look clippered but should be well blended.

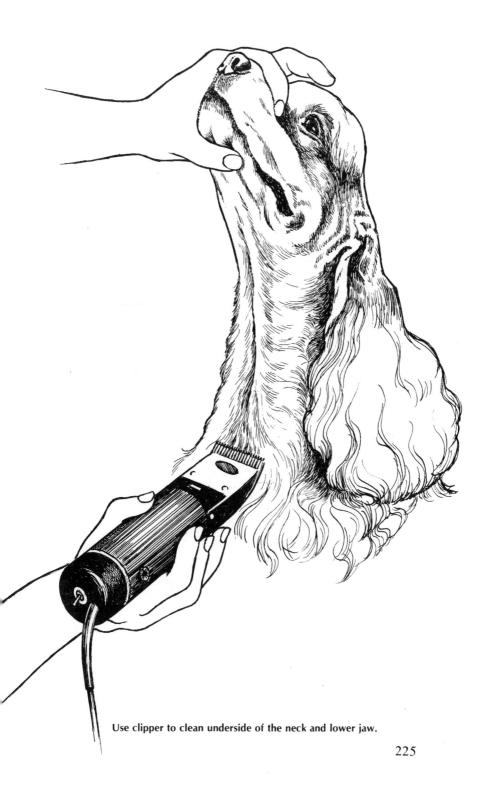

Use clipper to clean underside of the neck and lower jaw.

The next step and a very important one, is the bath. This may seem a simple procedure but there are certain steps one can take to enhance the appearance of the coat and prepare it for the final trimming.

This is the time to check the coat thoroughly for tangles and mats. If you find any, they should be pulled apart gently and then brushed with a pin brush. Do not use a wire or slicker brush for regular grooming as they tend to split the ends of the hair.

Many kinds of soap on the market today have a detergent base. For show dogs, where they are bathed very often, I prefer a shampoo that is without the detergent base. It does require more rinsing to remove all the soap. To finish with a creme rinse is good, and on blacks, a vinegar rinse will bring out lustre. Rinsing is most important, and the hair should be rinsed until the hair squeaks when pulled through the fingers.

In drying the coat, first remove all excess water with towels. The remainder of the drying is done with a blower type dryer. Brush the back coat with the hair so it will lay flat.

If you can train the dog to lie on his side during the next step, it is easier. Brush the sides and the legs up and away from you. Complete a layer of hair at a time until entirely dry. Then turn the dog to the other side and repeat the process.

Spray the coat lightly with a good coat dressing mixed with water and towel the dog. Comb the back coat straight back and the sides straight down. For proper toweling, I take a large bath towel and divide it in half. Hem the raw edge and use this end for around the neck. Pin with a large safety pin loosely around the neck. Be sure the towel is not touching the back coat at this point. Then tightly draw the towel over the back to the tail. Then pull the sides of the towel over the sides and pin underneath the dog about at the end of the rib cage. This should be tight. Leave this on until you are ready for your final scissoring.

SMOOTH HAIR BEFORE TOWEL GOES ON

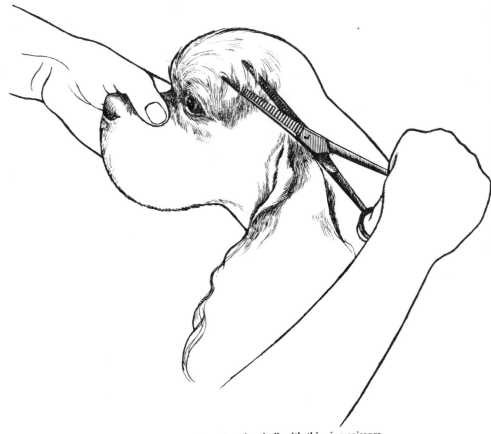

Trimming the skull with thinning scissors.

Now, for the final stage, the most difficult part of the head to trim is the skull. You must work for a clean look and yet a soft appearance. You have already placed a line across the back skull just above the occipital point. The remaining hair on top of the head must be thinned, using the fine thinners, until you have a soft, pleasing appearance. The difficult part is knowing just how much to leave. Remember, a flattened, hard look is not what you want. Neither do you want so much hair that it looks rough or unkempt. Use your thinners with the hair, never across it. Thin the long hair on top of the skull until it lays flat. Then blend the edges into the sides and into the line across the back skull.

228

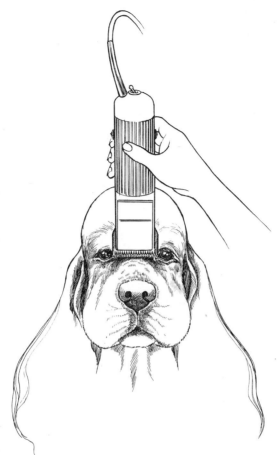

With a #15 blade clean out the stop with a reverse V.

Using the #15 blade, clean out the stop with a reverse V. If your dog is lacking in stop, clean out a reverse V but leave little tufts of hair on each side, close to the eye. This will give an impression of more stop than you actually have.

Go against the hair under the eyes and the sides of the cheek. This improves the chiseling. Then with the #10 blade, come forward against the hair on the top and sides of the muzzle. Stop before you reach the full part of the muzzle. This area is clipped with the clipper held out from the skin in order to keep the length of hair the dog might need. If the dog does not have as full a lip as you think he needs, a little hair will help. The fine thinnings shears are used to blend this excess hair into the muzzle. Do not make this look obvious or you defeat your purpose. The eyebrows and feelers on the brow must be scissored closely. The lashes should be trimmed to show off the Cocker's beautiful eyes. If you have an individual with lighter eyes than desirable, the lashes can be left a little longer.

229

Before the next work is started, have your dog in a posed position. You have already used the clippers to take off side hair to the shoulder muscle. Thin the hair on the back of the neck but some should remain to enhance the arch of the neck. There should be a smooth appearance though, with no stray ends protruding. The hair on each side is carefully blended into the part that has already been clipped.

Continue your scissoring going under the guard hair (the coarser, hard, shiny hair you find on the back) and with the lay of the coat—never across it. When you reach the shoulder muscle, lessen your scissoring as the shoulder must blend into the feathering of the front legs. When finished, the neck and shoulders should appear smooth and lean with all parts fitting together.

Work on the back coat is the next step. This varies because of different textures of coat. If you have a flat coat, you are fortunate. Simply check the dog's topline from the side and if there are any uneven places, thin from under the guard hair so the thinning is unnoticed. If the dog is a little high in the rear, thin as much as possible but still leave a thin coating of guard hair.

A fuzzy or curly type of coat presents more of a problem, particularly if the guard hair has been removed. The fuzz can be removed by using a coarse stripping knife or the side of your thinning shears with teeth. Go over the back coat with short strokes continually until the fuzz is removed. Since you have no guard hair with which to cover faults, you must wait for guard hair to come back.

230

Thinning the neck and back.

Thinning the tail area.

The back and flanks should have a very flat smooth look from the shoulder blades to the tail. Each side of the rump should be thinned sufficiently to blend into the feathering on the legs. Under the tail should be thinned almost to the hocks, blending as you thin. This will emphasize the angulation.

If your tail set is a little low and you have sufficient hair, you can build up the top of the tail to where the appearance of the tail is straight off the back. The Cocker should not have a skinned look to his tail. Remember, he is a sporting dog, not a terrier.

Before trimming the feet and checking the legs for further trimming, it is well to have someone gait your Cocker for you. Some faults in gaiting can be minimized with trimming. If your dog hocks in a bit, keep more feathering on the outside of the legs. Also move your dog a little slower as this will spread the hind legs to a certain extent. If he "paddles" (moving with his forefeet wide), thinning the feathering at the elbows will help.

The first thing to do in trimming the feet is to cut the nails and the hair from the bottom of the pads. Then stand the dog on the table and study the feet very carefully for imperfections and places for improvement by trimming. Toeing in or out can be helped greatly with trimming.

Use straight scissors, laying them on edge so the cut is perpendicular, not slanting. The size of the feet should conform to the amount of coat on the legs. If heavily feathered, a large round forefoot is attractive. If not so well feathered, the feet should not extend beyond the feathering.

The back feet are cut a little smaller than the front and any surplus hair hanging below the table level should be removed. To angle this upward looks well on heavy coated dogs. When your dog is finished, set him up in front of a mirror next to pictures of the show dogs you have been checking. Compare and improve where possible.

Using the armband to hold a comb.

12

How to Show
the Cocker Spaniel

SHOWING your own dog is a wonderful hobby and one
that I have always encouraged. The first thing you must do is to examine yourself. Decide whether you have the necessary patience. It
is well also to find if you have the gentle but firm hand to persuade
your Cocker to respond to your wishes and like it. In other words, if
you make a game of training for the show ring, your dog will be merry
and happy in what he is doing.

There is nothing so disconcerting to the judge and to yourself as seeing a Cocker with his tail down and looking very miserable in the show
ring. It is not only impossible to win with such a dog, but it certainly
gives a bad impression of Cocker temperament to the public.

The first thing you must teach your Cocker is to travel along by your
side on both a loose and semi-tight lead. Teach your dog to go on either
side. You will find correct procedure for lead training in the chapter on
Special Care and Training in this book.

Some have the impression that they must have natural talent to be
able to show their dog properly. While it does help a lot, one can learn.
It may mean working a little harder and longer as you must train yourself before you train the dog. Some who coordinate well are able to fall
right into correct handling. But even then, you first need to learn proper
procedure. You must be courteous always in the ring and subdue your
own inclination to "show off" simply because it comes easy.

If you are not fortunate enough to find this an easy procedure, then
you must start at the beginning. You must have a spirit of sports-

235

manship and be able to take your wins and losses in stride. Do not be kennel blind. All dogs have some faults and it will be up to you to learn of these faults and seek the help of an experienced person to try and minimize them.

Attend as many shows as you can and watch the Cocker ring. Watch procedure: how the professional handles his dog; how he puts on the lead and how he takes it off; how he gaits his dog and how he pays strict attention to the judge's wishes. Notice how the judge takes hold of the dog for examination. All these details will help you when you take the first leap and go into that ring.

Pose your dog often before a mirror with a picture of a top winner by your side. Imitate the pose and be sure to raise the head in the same manner. Practice makes perfect and it will soon become much easier to pose your dog properly.

One thing you must be sure about before you even think of entering a show is the physical condition of your Cocker. Is he in top coat? Is he in good weight — not fat and not thin? Is he free of external and internal parasites? Has he been groomed as outlined in the previous chapter? Is he clean? Has he received permanent DHL and rabies inoculations?

If you can answer in the affirmative to all of these questions, then try through other breeders to learn the whereabouts of some shows nearby. Learn the names of superintendents who operate in your vicinity and write to them for premium lists. These include entry blanks and the closing date for entry. This date is very important as no superintendent can take an entry after the closing date; or, if it is a limited show, he cannot take an entry after the posted limit is reached.

Of course, by this time your Cocker has been lead broken and taught to stand for examination by the judge. It is well to plan on taking a few things with you into the ring. You need a comb or brush and something for bait. You can use a piece of liver or a small toy (not too large) and if you have a pocket - fine. If not, your comb can be carried in your arm band as shown in the drawing. A small piece of liver can also be put inside the arm band.

It is well to practice holding your lead folded in your hand rather than having part of it hanging down. I prefer the Simplicity lead of the $\frac{3}{8}$ inch width. These come in various colors, but I prefer one that matches the color of the dog as near as possible. Your lead should not be conspicuous - remember above all, it is the dog you are showing.

At this point, I might mention your attire. Dress conservatively - do not overdress. Anything that will call attention of the judge away from the dog is not only bad taste but does not help you to win.

236

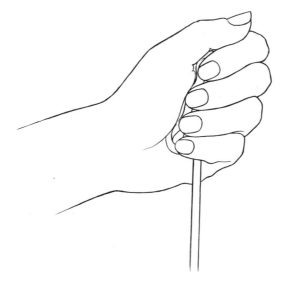

Lead properly held.

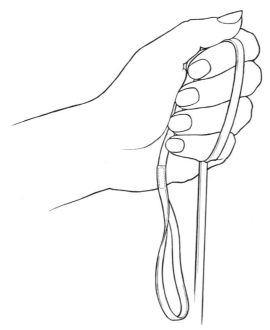

Lead improperly held.

There is even a right and a wrong way to place the lead on the neck (see drawings). Slip the lead over the head and bring it up directly behind the dog's ears. It should rest just under the jaw bones. With the lead in this position, the dog can gait with his head fairly erect and the arch showing nicely. One also has better control of the dog this way. If the lead is placed further down on the neck, you have little control and the dog lowers his head and completely loses style.

At this point, it is well to scan your competition. If your dog is on the small side, be careful not to drop in line between two large dogs. This will minimize the size of your dog. Likewise, if your dog is a bit large, look for the larger ones to try and follow. This is not always possible, but it is worth a try. Pick up your arm band early so you are ready for this manuver.

If you are showing a dog that really likes to "move out," it is well to try and get into the ring first. If you cannot do this and you find yourself behind a very slow moving dog that will not permit your dog to show to best advantage, hold your dog back as you go behind the judge and then let him out as you pass his viewpoint. If the dog in front of you stops, you are permitted to go around him. Above all, be ethical in your procedure.

Most judges take their class around the ring as soon as all entrants are present. When the line is stopped, immediately set up your dog, but allow plenty of room between your dog and the others. See that your dog is looking his very best as the judge passes along for that first glance. Often, a good-looking individual will catch his eye in that early stage of his evaluation.

Many judges today are judging on a table, so have your dog trained to stand steady on a table as well as on the floor. Watch the judge very closely for his procedure. Some judges prefer the owner or handler to show him the teeth so he can check the bite. If you have watched his preceding classes, you will know if he prefers this or if he opens the dog's mouth himself to check teeth.

While the judge is going over the front part of your dog, hold him firmly in the rear. When the judge shows by his actions that he is finished with the front end, move around and hold your dog firmly from the front. Pull the ears forward at this point so he can note the neck and shoulders better.

During this examination, it is well to have the loop that goes over the neck over your arm. When the judge motions everyone up for further gaiting, you are ready to slip the lead over the dog's head in a hurry. However, do not forget to place your lead in the proper place, well up under the chin, before you start to gait.

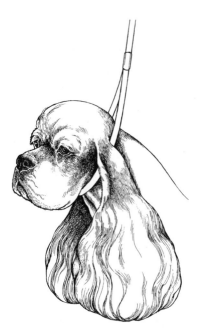

Lead placed correctly on neck.

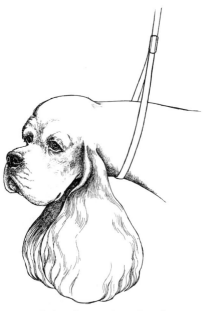

Lead placed on neck too loosely.

Judges have different patterns of gaiting the dogs. If possible, watch the preceding classes to ascertain his wishes. Some judges prefer the dog going straight down and across the end and returning the same way. This is called an "L." Others like the "triangle" pattern which I prefer and that is straight down, across the end and back on the center mat. This saves time and still gives the judge a view from every side. The sketch will show this procedure.

If your dog is well enough trained, after you have followed the judge's instruction to go straight down and back or to gait in an "L" or a triangle, and you bring the dog back to the judge, let him stand a few seconds facing the judge. If he has a particularly beautiful head, and lovely eyes, this is bound to make an impression.

The general condition of your Cocker is something you should consider. He may be beautiful and have a lovely coat, but if he is soft when pressure is applied, many judges will consider him "out of condition". Whether he is a show dog or a pet, his exercising should not be neglected.

At one time, when our show dogs were being shown in the ring every week and we had a string of eight or more, they were taken (two at a time) and walked two miles a day. These dogs were kept in the pink of condition and were hard as nails. This also familiarized the dogs with noises and people. The younger your Cocker is when you begin this training, the easier it will be for both you and the Cocker, and he will adjust to your wishes in every way.

While you may think this represents a lot of work, and perhaps it does, the reward makes it worthwhile. The best tonic for conditioning is good food and plenty of exercise.

Weigh your dog when you feel he is in correct weight and then try and keep him in that same weight. If he gets a little fat, cut down on the amount of food given. Likewise, if he appears a bit on the thin side, increase the amount of food accordingly.

One of the reasons conditioning and training are so important is the limited time the judge has for evaluating each dog. If the dog is well trained and cooperates with the judge and the handler, he can be checked over in a short time. If he does not cooperate and does not hold for examination, the judge may pass on to the next dog with little or no evaluation of the untrained dog.

There are some faults that I consider more difficult to correct than others, even with selective breeding. It has been my experience that length of back or coupling is one of the most difficult places in which to attain perfection through selective breeding. I believe it is easier to

240

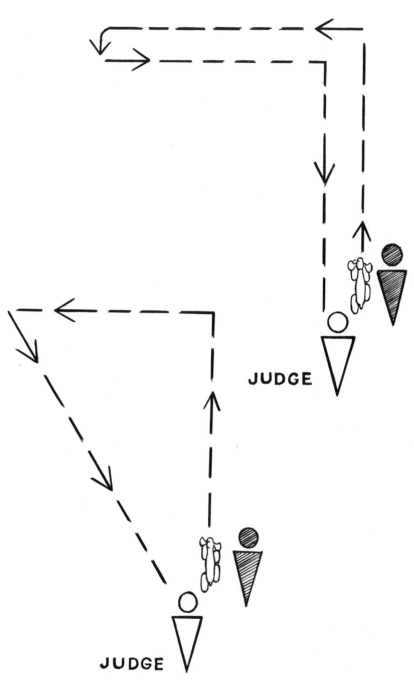

JUDGE

JUDGE

Gaiting patterns.
Top, "L" pattern. Lower, triangle pattern.

improve heads, rears or even neck and shoulders. If one attempts to shorten coupling by breeding to a short backed individual, there is the possibility of losing the space needed for freedom of movement.

A long backed dog is usually a good moving dog. However, he is usually hard to pose with a good topline and very often will have a slight dip at the end of the rib cage. It is not easy to obtain the perfection needed to hold a good topline and still have sufficient length of loin to give the free movement that is desirable.

There is a tendency among some exhibitors and handlers to hold the dog's tail straight up like a terrier. This is usually the case where a dog has a long back. While it may shorten the appearance a little, it is still not the correct tail carriage for the Cocker. The Standard says *"straight off the back or slightly higher, but never straight up like a terrier"*.

Proper gaiting is another very important procedure. Many good judges make their final decision on the movement of the dog. I feel that it is important for breeders and exhibitors to be aware of the reasons for imperfections in gait and movement. While fancy dictates that some breeds be judged specifically on certain features such as head or coat, with little emphasis on movement, this is not true of the Cocker Spaniel. He is a sporting dog and sporting dogs must be able to move correctly.

We sometimes hear the remark about a certain dog, "He is a beautiful dog posed but he falls apart on the lead." Again, we hear the statement, "If a dog is put together right, he must move right." It would seem the two statements are inconsistent, and the latter, in my opinion, should be reversed. "If a dog moves right, he MUST be put together right." Certainly, if we find perfection in movement, we will find perfection in conformation, as far as the running gear is concerned.

Angulation is generally considered one of the important proponents to proper gaiting. What is meant by angulation? It is a bend between the shoulder blade and the upper arm of the front legs, and a bend between the upper and lower thighs at the stifle joint of the hindquarters. Most certainly correct balance in the angulation, fore and rear, has a decided effect on movement.

We sometimes see a dog in the ring that obviously has excellent rear angulation with the desired well let down hocks, and should have drive and smoothness when gaiting. But, when the dog moves he loses balance and the parts do not seem to fit together as one unit. Why is this? While the rear angulation seems perfect, the front angulation undoubtedly is lacking and this throws the entire picture out of balance.

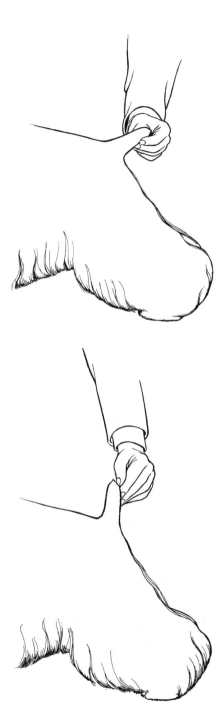

Correct tail placement.

Tail being held too high.

The pride of winning.

Surprising as it may seem, a dog with a mediocre front and a mediocre rear that are in balance, one with the other, will produce better results in movement than a beautifully angulated rear on a dog with stilted shoulder blades. The reverse can be the case where a dog with the 45% layback is coupled with a straight rear.

A good normal gait viewed from the side is timed so that the front leg moves just ahead of the back leg. In other words, the front pad is lifted to get out of the way of the back pad and the faster the gait, the more necessary perfection of this action becomes.

Coupling, length of body, well-laid back shoulders and rear angulation all have a decided effect upon this correct normal gait. If the body is too short, the stride too long, or the timing incorrect, the dog will have to sidestep or he may move crab-like. This also can bring about the side-winding of some dogs.

The reasons for the many imperfections that appear, not only in the Cocker, but in all purebred dogs, present a challenge to breeders. Perfection has yet to be seen but some of the beautiful Cockers seen in the ring today can only mean we are coming close.

Some dogs, including the Cocker, will occasionally fall into a pace and this gait is condemned by the dog folks though it is accepted by the horse people. To pace means that both legs on each side move in unison. When the left front leg moves, so does the left rear, and the same with the right side. A dog that falls into a pace frequently is faulty. I have found a fat dog or one out of condition will sometimes pace. Lack of muscle tone is sometimes reflected by pacing. A dog out of balance in angulation will often pace, and a tired, weary dog will pace.

A good gaiting Cocker should move with a smooth trot, with a free, swinging action, plenty of shoulder and stifle movement and with no sign of stilted nor hackney action. It is a beautiful sight to see a smooth moving Cocker, or rather three, in a Sporting Group holding their own in speed, and looking every bit the true sporting breed they are.

Check your dog's movement carefully and do not be kennel blind. Find out his faults and through selective breeding, endeavor to improve them.

Tom O'Neal with four youngsters – all
finished to their championships later.

13

Care and Training
of the Cocker Spaniel

The CARE of the Cocker Spaniel covers many things: daily feeding; personal attention including grooming; training for proper behavior, at home, on the street and in the show ring; constant check for external and internal parasites and for any other ailments or irregularities that might appear.

The care of a Cocker Spaniel should begin early in his life, when just a puppy. It is well to take every precaution to assure yourself of the sturdiness and health of the puppy if it is one that you are purchasing. If it is one that you have whelped and raised from birth, you should be equally careful of his health. Remember, too, that a dog may have constitutional vigor without breed type, but ideally you should seek both. A vital, desirable dog is one that is easy to raise and is worth the care and effort that is bestowed upon him.

Coat Care

The Cocker is by nature a clean dog, so make every effort to see that your facilities permit him to remain clean. If you do your part, you'll find him a dog to cherish.

Generations of love of Cockers. Mrs. Betty Schachner with her mother
(Minerva Purcell) and her daughter Lisa, and five of their Spaniels.

I want to stress the point that you cannot have your dog in full coat if you neglect to groom and bathe him when needed. This should be done at least a couple of times a week to avoid the heavy mats that will form, particularly during the shedding season. There is nothing so disheartening as to see a heavy coated Cocker whose full coat has become one solid mat. This leads to skin problems, bad sores and becomes a nesting place for external parasites.

These pests are particularly bad in the summertime and come from so many sources they are even found on our "best-bred" dogs. However, this doesn't have to be the case as there are many excellent materials today that will completely eliminate them.

Cleanliness is very necessary and flea collars have proven very helpful, particularly in the larger kennels where it is difficult to go over the entire kennel daily with a dip or spray. There is a very good "Kennel Dust" available which can be scattered in the runs and also in the area surrounding the kennel. In many locations, constant care is needed during the hot weather.

Skin disorders can become a real problem with the heavy coats of Cockers and very often the owner is not aware of these conditions until they become a serious matter. This probably keeps the veterinarians busier than any other ailment because it is difficult to find the cause quickly and then it is a slow procedure to heal.

Scratching is usually the first indication of trouble and when one finds the scratching is not caused by external parasites, it is well to check with your veterinarian to find the cause. This is not always easy even with the fine vets we have today. Diet is usually checked first and is often the cause. A nervous dog will sometimes scratch for no reason and it could be that the dog is allergic to something he comes in constant contact with such as a rug.

The capable veterinarian will make all sorts of tests in his efforts to find out the reason and this takes time. In the meantime your dog keeps on scratching and tearing his coat apart. What is the answer? Frequent grooming and cleanliness are the best answers. If one finds a skin irritation early, it is just a small problem to clear it up before it becomes serious. Usually, a salve from your vet will do the trick.

Internal parasites also present a problem. A check for worms should be made from time to time through the analysis of stool specimens by the veterinarian. There is also the problem of heartworm in some areas and this can be a serious problem. This check should be made every spring and if negative a medication can be given during the summer months that will help avoid heartworm infection.

Grooming the Pet

While the Cocker Spaniel is a very hardy dog and can hold his own in the field, fashion has dictated that he have a beautiful and profuse coat. If your dog is your pet and you prefer not to groom him daily, it is possible to trim the coat in what I have named a "Suburban Clip." This consists of cutting the leg feathering and the belly coat to about 2 inches in length.

The back can be kept smooth and close, also neck and shoulders. The head can be trimmed just like a show dog. The ears can be clipped down about 3 inches from the top and the rest of the ear left the full length.

This will give you a Cocker resembling a half grown puppy and is a very attractive clip. It is easy to care for and for those who are not dedicated to daily grooming, it works exceptionally well.

If you like to take your dog to the country and let him run in the field and woods, this clip is particularly desirable. If burrs and twigs are caught in the coat, they are much easier to remove with the short coat and do not become entangled in long strands as they would with the full coat.

Another part of the Cocker that needs attention often are the eyes. The Cocker eyes are large and exposed to dust and particles in the air. This can cause a little secretion to drip from the eyes. This will form a little crust and on the lighter colored dogs, will cause a stain. If a good eye wash is used a couple of times a week, this can be avoided. Use wet cotton to wipe the edges. The beauty of his eyes are an important part of the Cocker's heritage.

The Cocker's ears are so long and hang so closely to his head that little air gets into them. If neglected, wax forms, and the first thing you know, you have cankers. These can become very serious and chronic. I use a preparation called Earguard and my Cockers' ears are cleaned out about twice a week. In this way, I avoid dirty, cankerous ears which are the bane of so many Cocker owners.

Another thought about ears which I learned from my family doctor many years ago—never use a Q-tip or any stick with cotton on the end. I use my finger and wrap cotton around it. In this way you cannot go so far down as to cause an injury. Many a canker started up in this way.

If you trim your own pet and take care of his needs, do not forget the nails. If they have gotten too long, I suggest taking just a small amount

250

The three Cockers pictured indicate the tendency during the 1960s to show with heavy coats. These dogs were bred and owned by Bernice Toney and did some nice winning in their time. However, the excessive care that was necessary to groom them is easily seen. Today, Cockers being prepared for the show ring are generally given a smoother, cleaner appearance. The standard now clearly states: "Well feathered but not so excessively as to hide the Cocker Spaniel's true lines and movement or affect his appearance and function as a Sporting dog." There are some breeders, unfortunately, who are still trying for coat and more coat. Their reasoning is that they cannot win without a heavy coat. In some cases this is true – so perhaps it's more a matter of educating our judges.

Cocker in Suburban Clip.

251

off each week. If the nail is white, you can easily see the quick so just take off the white part. If the nail is black, more care must be taken so if a little is taken off each week, you can be sure you are not going too far. If you make a mistake and the nail bleeds, do not get alarmed. Get some *Quick-stop* from your pet shop and this will soon stop the bleeding.

Also, trim your dog's pads and the bottom of the feet. When this mats, it forms little hard balls and can be very painful for your dog to walk on. Sometimes these cause the pad to become inflamed and quite red. My suggestion in this case is to soak the feet in an epsom salt solution. This is antiseptic and also toughen the pads.

On either side of the anus of the dog is situated an anal gland, which secretes a lubricant that better enables the dog to expel the contents of the rectum. These glands often become clogged and a fetid mass accumulates in them. This can be removed by seizing the tail with the left hand, encircling the base with the thumb and forefinger of the right hand and pressing the anus firmly between thumb and finger. A semiliquid of vile odor is extruded from the anus. This should be repeated about once a month.

Summer Care

It has been said that dogs require proportionately more air for breathing than do human beings and, as a dog perspires through his tongue and pads, he will be affected by the heat more quickly than humans. For this reason it is well to park your car in the shade and leave not just one, but two or three windows open for cross ventilation. If you open them just two or three inches, it will not be enough to permit your dog to escape and it may save his life.

It is well when leaving a dog alone in the car to remove his lead as it is possible for a lead to become entangled in the steering wheel when the dog jumps from the front to the back of the car. He could be badly injured in this way.

Summer eczema is not uncommon among dogs and is usually caused by the dog's diet. Check with your veterinarian at the first sign and endeavor to have the diet corrected.

Stripping a coat completely down to the skin does not make your dog any cooler, for the coat serves as insulation against heat in sum-

252

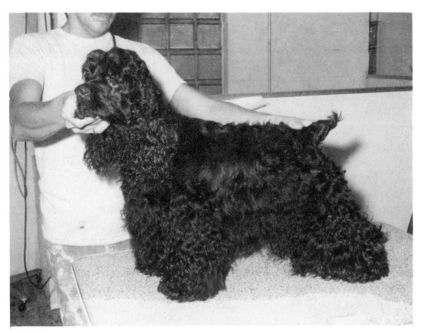

Today's Cocker in the rough.

Same Cocker after trimming for show.

253

mer and cold in winter. The stripping exposes him to insects, parasites, etc. as well as the heat. This is a warning that is probably not needed by the show-minded fancier but it is amazing how many breeders completely strip down their kennel stock for easier care.

Feeding Your Cocker

The amount to be fed to young puppies, growing youngsters and mature dogs, depends entirely on the size and age of the individual. I do not believe in overfeeding but I like to see a well-rounded stomach, particularly on the youngsters. However, this does not mean a distended stomach.

Puppies up to four months of age should be fed four times a day. From four months to six months of age, three feedings should be sufficient. From six months to a year, twice a day and from then on, it depends on their condition. Mature dogs are fed their main meal in the late afternoon with a small snack in the morning.

After Cockers are off their puppy diet their feeding for the rest of their lives is pretty much the same. This diet rarely changes unless an unusual condition arises. It consists of one-third ground beef, either raw or cooked; one-third small kibble and one-third a rather fine commercial meal. The addition of vitamins and calcium is important for bitches in whelp or if another weakness exists. Vitamins A and D are usually given to bitches during their entire period of pregnancy, and until puppies are weaned.

Common sense must be used in your feeding operations. If dogs are thin, they should receive two full meals a day. If too fat, they receive one rather light meal a day until reduced to correct weight. For tidbits I use a commercial food that comes in small pieces. It is well to try several brands until you find one that the dogs relish.

Care of the Stud Dog and Brood Bitch

Proper care and handling of the stud dog is also very important. This is necessary if he is to maintain his vitality and good condition. This is particularly true if he is a popular stud and is used frequently.

Diet should not be a problem. The same good nourishing diet that is required in order to keep any dog or bitch in top condition, is all that is required. We use the same diet that is given to our bitches. However, it is the belief of our veterinarian that, for the stud dog, there is plenty of Vitamin E present in a well balanced diet and a further addition of this vitamin can upset the hormone balance of the

254

body. We do add a piece of suet to this diet as it seems to improve the condition of the coat.

A busy stud dog should be given plenty of exercise and plenty of fresh air. This is where the stud who is being shown and confined to a crate a good part of the time, might suffer. Such dogs should be exercised by the handler in the open air at every opportunity. Though plenty of exercise is important, it should not take place immediately following a mating when a stud should be kept very quiet and confined for a period. This is particularly true in hot weather.

There is also the question of how often a stud should be used in order to maintain his well-being and keep him an eager, active stud. We have found that not more than twice a week is the best schedule. If used twice in one week, it is well, if possible, to rest him the following week. I know some breeders and handlers differ with this idea and use their studs much more often. If they check, they may find that there are more than an average of misses for this stud. Misses are not always the fault of the bitch. If bitches are carefully checked and bred at the right time, but one service is needed.

The safe and competent handling of bitches shipped in to be bred, is the responsibility of the owner or handler. There must be safe quarters, clean and secure, for their housing. They must be carefully watched so they are bred at the right time. Some use the test tape method and others get a check by their veterinarian, which in our mind is the safest way.

It is also the responsibility of the owner or handler of an advertised stud to have that dog in top condition and be positive of his fertility at all times. This is equally important in regard to those stud dogs who have been retired from the show ring.

A stud dog, whether a popular one or one that is just used occasionally, should not be a hot-house plant; he should not be pampered and coddled, but given every opportunity to be a rugged individual and live a normal, healthy life. In return, he will sire many healthy litters, providing, of course, the bitches brought to him are equally healthy, normal individuals.

Training Your Pet

Regardless of the breed, the way a young puppy is played with in his early life can have a lasting influence on his behavior. Aggressive tendencies may easily develop because of such a seemingly small matter as holding out a bone or a toy, and then snatching it away just as the pup is about to take it. Teasing tricks in play are all too common, especially with children who do not realize that it is a bad practice and could cause your pup to become defensive and surly. Parents should see to it that this does not happen.

Many owners (as well as some trainers and handlers) could do with some training themselves before undertaking to train their Cockers. Rough treatment is not the way. While the Cocker is a sturdy dog, he is also a sensitive dog. When he does wrong, just a cross word will usually bring him in hand. If you clearly let him know what you want, and all the members of the family or the kennel do so in like manner, the dog will respond. However if one person is rough in his treatment of the dog when he makes a mistake, and another just laughs it off, the Cocker becomes confused and the trouble begins.

As with most dogs, the Cocker is a creature of habit. If he is taught good habits, they will stay with him during his life. If he is allowed to pick up bad habits, they are sometimes difficult to change.

The puppy is never too young to start training. Whether it is housebreaking, lead breaking, control of barking, or whatever—the earlier you start the better trained your dog will become.

The house training of the Cocker is something that should be started at an early age—three months is not too soon. The Cockers are naturally clean dogs and prefer to stay that way if given a chance. Early training on newspaper is good. Most kennels keep their pups on newspaper for the first few weeks of their life so they are accustomed to this training from the start. Keep the pup in a certain area when you bring him home. Do not let him run through the house unless you are right there: To him your beautiful rugs are the same as grass. If he makes a mistake, unless you catch him in the act, please do not chastise him as he does not know the reason for his punishment.

Take the pup outdoors often and usually to the same spot. I have found that taking the soiled newspaper out and anchoring it with a couple of stones soon becomes his place to exercise. Then the paper can be removed and he will still prefer to go to that particular place.

Early training on the lead is good. First, place a light collar on his neck and let him go around with the collar on for a few days. Then attach a short lead to this collar and let him pull that around. This procedure will get him used to something around his neck. It will then be much easier to put a loose slip lead on him and take him about on that.

Use no pressure until he becomes accustomed to the loose lead. Then, slowly lift his head, using something for bait if necessary. Make a game of it and praise him when he has completed his walk.

Further training is discussed in the chapter on Obedience.

The Comfort of Your Cocker

It is not unusual for Cockers, young and old, to want to sleep about half the time. This is considered normal and to be expected. Their regular sleeping time is during the night with many daytime naps. However, they awaken quickly at any hour and are ready for your attention and a romp.

The comfort of your Cockers is entirely in your hands. It is much easier to keep them in top condition than to neglect them and then attempt to restore good condition in a hurry. A half-hour with the brush every day will keep out the mats. Usually, a bath once a week is sufficient. Unless you have a very heavy coated dog, trimming once a month will suffice. Of course, if he is going to a dog show, that is something different.

If the dogs are suffering from heat or cold, it is entirely the fault of the owner or handler. It is up to the owner or handler to be sure the dogs are comfortable. Dogs do show their appreciation in many ways for anything you can do to make them more comfortable.

Today's Cocker, in many cases, is definitely a member of the family. His place is in the home. With proper training, he is completely housebroken and as clean as any other member of the family. His schedule should be as exacting as that of a baby.

This is also true with breeders, raising litters for sale or for show. Dogs, today, are scientifically raised and cared for. They are trained—some for the show ring, some for obedience work, some for field work and a great majority for a place in a home where he can prove a companion and provide great pleasure for the entire family.

Three generations of Obedience Cockers owned by Mary Lee Whiting: Marly's Harvest Queen, UD; Mar Lee's Air O'Blarney, UD; and Mar Lee's Wee Bit O'Blarney, UD.

258

14

The Cocker Spaniel in Obedience

by John S. Ward

IT is axiomatic that all dogs should be trained. Without some form of basic training, a dog is not under control and is no better than a wild animal. This holds true regardless of the ultimate use to which a dog may be put, whether he is to be a pet, a show dog, a police or a military dog.

Basic training is usually considered to include heeling, which is walking quietly on leash, staying in one place until released, and coming when called. Additionally, the dog should learn to sit, to lie down, and to stand on command.

Once the dog has been brought under control, the more specialized training required for a specific function is begun. To those who are dog show oriented, this generally consists of training him for either conformation or obedience competition, or perhaps both. Since conformation showing is fully discussed elsewhere, this section will be devoted to the formal aspect of obedience training known as Obedience Trials, and will attempt to give the Cocker owner who is interested in such competition some idea of the factors involved in the sport.

Obedience Trials are events sanctioned by the American Kennel Club, where dogs may, by passing a series of increasingly difficult tests, be awarded Obedience titles, just as dogs shown in conformation may be designated Champion. These titles are Companion Dog (abbreviated C.D.), Companion Dog Excellent (C.D.X), and Utility Dog (U.D.). Requirements for these titles may be obtained by writing the American Kennel Club and asking for their publication "Obedience Regulations."

The role of the Cocker Spaniel in the sport of dog obedience goes back to the very beginning of obedience itself. In fact, three of the ten contestants in the first obedience "test" held in conjunction with an all-breed dog show were Cocker Spaniels. The event was the North Westchester Kennel Club show held in Mount Kisco, N.Y., on June 9, 1934.

This early identification of the Cocker Spaniel with dog obedience is not hard to understand. The emergence of this form of competition coincided with the rise in popularity of the Cocker in the late thirties and early forties. Also, the skills necessary for successful obedience training (heeling, staying, coming when called and retrieving) are quite similar to those taught to bird dogs for field work, and Cockers had been bred for these attributes from their beginnings. Finally, the Cocker is usually a willing obedience pupil and is highly motivated to please his handler, so the training is usually successful.

The American Spaniel Club has long recognized the importance of obedience, and has held an Obedience Trial in conjunction with its annual national specialty for many years. In addition, it has awarded an annual trophy for the Spaniel accumulating the most points in qualifying scores at obedience trials for that year. It also offered a $500 savings bond for the first Cocker dual title holder in the areas of breed, field or obedience.

Temperament

Since temperament is such an important factor in dog training, it is worth going into the subject in depth.

One of the questions most often asked of dog trainers is "What is the most important quality in determining a dog's trainability?" The unhesitating answer is his temperament. We can define temperament as the way in which a dog reacts to his environment and all of its ingredients such as things, people, noises, smells, and even other dogs. Of these, the most important single aspect is how he reacts to people, since he is a domestic animal, and must put up with us.

There is no doubt as to what sort of temperament we are looking for

Ch. Tabaka's Tres Jolie, UD, owned by Ruth Tabaka.

. Tabaka's Tammy Tan Toes,)T. Shown finishing her Utility e the day after she finished for r championship.

261

in our Cockers. The breed standard says *"Above all he must be free and merry, sound, well-balanced throughout, and in his action show a keen inclination to work; equable in temperament, with no suggestion of timidity."* We are, therefore, looking for a tail-wagging, merry dog, who is everybody's friend.

There has been much debate on the effect of heredity on dog temperaments, but recent studies have rather clearly demonstrated that there are significant differences in the behavior of dogs which are traceable to heredity. We are indeed fortunate, in the words of one behaviorist, that "The Cocker is born liking people; he is born almost socialized to human beings." This inheritance accounted for the Cocker's tremendous popularity in years gone by, but unfortunately, it also led to indiscriminate breeding that almost undid this marvelous temperament. However, the numerical popularity of the Cocker went down sharply some time ago, and now that he is moving up the ladder again, breeding for the most part is in the hands of the serious breeder.

It is in the field of molding a dog's temperament by manipulating his environment, however, that the owner can do most to insure sound temperament. There is a period of socialization in puppies which lasts from about four weeks to about twelve weeks of age, during which time a dog's attitude toward human beings is to be a large extent fixed. In other words, the greater variety of pleasant experiences with humans a puppy can have in his early life, the sounder temperamentally he will be.

Within the general category of temperament, a specific quality that becomes exceedingly important in training is the dog's motivation. Unlike all other animals, the training of dogs depends entirely on their desire to please humans, which fortunately Cockers have in abundance. It is not necessary to bribe the dog with food nor to use force or brutality. All that is required is to communicate to him what you want him to do, correct him when he makes mistakes, and praise him when he does it right.

A person attempting to train a Cocker usually has only himself to blame if the training doesn't take, since the dog is very anxious to please. Along with this characteristic, however, is another quality the Cocker has which affects his response to training techniques, and that is his susceptibility to getting discouraged if his trainer is heavy-handed. The training had better be cheerful and full of encouragement if you are to get the most out of your Cocker.

Motivation is quite important when teaching a dog to carry out a non-instinctive action. In this category fall such activities as staying in one place when left, or heeling close to a handler. Desire to please is

Mar Lee's Kiss O'Blarney, UD.

less important in training the dog in such activities as finding birds or animals for hunting purposes, since these tendencies are born in the dog, and usually need only to be cultivated and channeled. Again, however, we must realize that what is instinctive for one breed or even an individual in that breed may be missing in another. Retrieving is such an activity.

Training for Obedience Trials

The Cocker owner who wishes to obedience train his dog has basically three alternatives: have it trained by a professional trainer, train it out of a book, or attend a training class. By far the best course is the latter, and fortunately dog training classes are easily found in most parts of the country.

263

Ch. Ward's Tidy Contribution, UD, a beautiful representative of Cockers owning both conformation and Obedience titles. Pictured going Winners enroute to 1968 championship. Bred and owned by Mr. and Mrs. John S. Ward.

Dog training classes usually have two objectives: to offer basic dog training to the public for simple control purposes, and to conduct a program of advanced obedience training in preparation for showing dogs in obedience trials. Fortunately, all dogs are given the same basic training, regardless of the ultimate goal of the handler, so these objectives are totally compatible. As a matter of fact, most people in a basic dog training class have never heard of obedience trials, and become interested only by virtue of exposure to the advanced work.

There are many advantages to training your Cocker in a class. Since training is a physical activity, the owner is instructed in the proper form for teaching the dog various exercises, which is sometimes difficult to pick up by reading a book. Additionally, it gives the owner/handler the opportunity to discuss his problems with the instructor. Finally, and most important from the dog's point of view, it accustoms him to working in the presence of other dogs.

One must, nevertheless, be cautious in the selection of a class. It is wise to check out their credentials with knowledgeable dog people in the area, such as breeders and veterinarians. The class should be

264

visited before signing up, to be sure the atmosphere is generally business-like and cheerful and that the training methods are acceptable. If you are interested in ultimately showing in obedience trials, it is important that the group have an advanced training program that can take you as far as desired. Generally speaking, if you are interested in competition, you are wise to seek out a club that not only holds classes, but also puts on obedience trials.

This is not to imply that there are no good training books available. There are many excellent ones, written by acknowledged experts, but the authors would probably be the first to agree that there is no substitute for a class. Your dog will ultimately be called to perform in a ring at an obedience trial, so he had better get used to the atmosphere early in his career.

Conformation vs. Obedience

The question of the compatibility of breed and obedience competition with the same dog has been raised many times in the past, and will be argued many times in the future. Unfortunately, the arguments on both sides can result from misinformation, rather than information, and in many cases the debaters have not thought the problem through. There is no simple yes/no answer to the question, and usually the facts in each individual case must be known before it can be determined whether a particular dog can be trained for both types of competition.

First of all, it must be appreciated that *all* dog showing involves training, be it breed or obedience. It is necessary, for example, to know whether the same person will be teaching the dog both types of performance, and even more important, does that person know how to train dogs for both.

Equally significant is how patient (or impatient) is the trainer in achieving his objectives. It would be ill-advised, for example, to show the average dog in the breed ring while he's in the middle of a basic obedience course. The dog has not sorted out in his mind what he is supposed to do, and he is bound to be confused if conflicting demands are made of him when he is going through the beginning Obedience process.

The method of Obedience training must also be taken into account. Fortunately, most obedience schools these days are just as interested in producing dogs that work cheerfully as are breeders and handlers. On the other hand, the quality of the instruction is important, and the

265

dog can wind up being trained for neither obedience nor breed in the hands of incompetent or unimaginative instructors. Ideally, the class should be conducted by individuals who are equally at home in the breed or Obedience ring.

With all these principles in mind, it becomes possible to consider specific situations. For example, ours is a breed that very often matures early, and a young dog may very well be ready for conformation showing. If you are going to put such a young dog with a handler, there is probably not much point in starting his obedience training in any sort of formal fashion before he starts his breed career. If for no other reason, the dog will probably board with the handler, and the owner will not have the opportunity to follow through with the daily practice that is necessary to groove the dog in his training.

Also, obedience training is probably out of the question for an individual who is deeply involved in an extensive breeding and showing program. It's usually simply a question of lack of time to do both. There are exceptions of course, and several of our successful large-scale breeders have done both, but it requires dedication.

The most satisfactory combination of these forms of competition is usually found in the case of the modest-scale breeder who has only one or two dogs being shown at a time, and who does his own training and showing. As a matter of fact, obedience training is an excellent way for the newcomer to learn to techniques of working with dogs, so that he acquires assurance in his actions when he has a dog at the end of a lead.

It might be useful to discuss certain specific techniques involved in training a dog that is to be shown in both breed and obedience. It is very helpful, at least in the early stages, to use a training or slip collar when teaching heeling, to permit corrections when the dog makes a mistake, and to use a show-lead when training him to gait. This helps him differentiate between the two in the beginning, although it is unnecessary when he is fully trained, since he will then take his cues from your voice and manner of handling. (A nylon slip collar can be used in teaching heeling if you are concerned about the effect of a chain collar on his coat.) It is also advisable to practice both gaiting and heeling at the same session, so he clearly understands these are two different things. Above all, remember that heeling is essentially a cheerful exercise, and that encouragement and praise are what make a tail-wagging, attentive heeler, not over-use of the training collar.

With regard to teaching the dog to sit when you halt in heeling, and to remain standing when he stops gaiting in the breed ring, this can be accomplished by the judicious selection of training techniques. The method is relatively simple, but requires practice and patience. When

Ch. Tabaka's Tidbit O'Wynden, CDX, the most spectacular of the many Cockers of Tabaka prefix that have starred in both conformation and Obedience. After setting quite a show record in the West under the handling of Jim Hall (with whom she is shown here), Tidbit is at this writing winning Bests in Show and Groups in the East under Ted Young's guidance. She was Best in Show at the 1978 ASC National Specialty. Co-owned by Ruth Tabaka and Laura Watt O'Connor.

you halt in heeling, stop in place, facing forward, and give the dog the command "Sit," while putting him in a sitting position with your left hand. If you wish him to stand when you stop, as in the breed ring, he is taught to do so as an obedience exercise at first, using the training collar and lead. To make him stand upon halting, make a quarter-turn to the left in place as you stop, so that you are facing the dog, extend your right arm with the lead so that the dog is stopped away from your side, and tell him to "Stand." It may be necessary in the early training to use your left hand in front of his right hind leg to block him in the standing position and to keep him from sitting. With practice, he will sit

267

whenever you stop in place facing forward, and will stand whenever you stop and turn so as to face him. What's more, the motion of your body will serve as the signal, and no oral command will be necessary. The virtue of this method is that your quarter-turn to the left is the natural motion you make in the breed ring when stopping the dog in front of the judge at the conclusion of gaiting.

Above all, do not enroll in an obedience class and then announce that you do not intend to make the dog sit when you come to halt in heeling, because you have a "breed" dog. The hackles of the instructors will rise because you are announcing that neither you nor they can train the dog to either sit or stand as the occasion demands. Surely we are smarter than that.

Posing, of course, is simply a "Stand-stay." The dog must be trained to pose while undergoing a breed examination, and he must literally be examined as part of his practice in basic obedience training. An obedience class, incidentally, is the ideal place to get your Cocker thoroughly accustomed to being examined.

Tracking

No discussion of obedience would be complete without reference to tracking. The American Kennel Club will issue a Tracking Dog certificate and will permit the use of the letters "T.D." after the name of a dog which has been certified by two judges at a tracking test as having passed, provided at least three dogs actually participated. The tests are separately held, and are not given at a dog show or an obedience trial.

The test consists of the dog following the track of a stranger not less than a quarter-mile, and no less than a half-hour old, and finding a glove or wallet belonging to the stranger which is left at the end of the track. The track includes at least two right-angle turns. The dog wears a harness to which is attached a leash between 20 and 40 feet in length.

It has been estimated that a dog's nose is about 400 times more sensitive than a human's, and thus every dog is born knowing how to track. Indeed, a large part of his activities in life consists of tracking, as witness his busy nose when he is turned loose in the backyard. The challenge, therefore, lies in teaching him to identify and follow the specific track you wish him to follow, and then motivating him to follow that track exclusively, without being distracted by the scent of animals, birds, or even other people.

Tracking enthusiasts constitute a small but intensely dedicated portion of the dog fancy. Like field trials, tracking tests give the dog an opportunity to do what is instinctive with him, and he enjoys himself tremendously when on track. Teaching a dog to track requires a strong motivation on the part of the handler too, expecially in metropolitan areas of the country, where adequate open space for tracking is hard to find.

Some Notable Obedience Cockers

In the early days of obedience competition, most of the Cocker Spaniels that competed successfully in advanced obedience work came out of New England. The first five Cocker Spaniels to complete the requirements for a Utility Dog (U.D.) title were: Llenroc Tops, owned by Dana B. Jefferson Jr. of Wellesley, Mass. (1940); Boots Biggs, owned by Robert F. Biggs of Dedham, Mass. (1941); Dusky Lady VII, from Providence, Rhode Island, owned by H. Stanton Smith (1941); Pudgington of Big Heart, of Cleveland, Ohio, owned by Mr. and Mrs. R. N. Grondie (1941); and Trayken Traveler, owned by Richard W. Crafts, of Wellesley, Mass. (1942).

While the Cocker has demonstrated his versatility in all phases of dog competition, there are not as many instances of competition across the board as one might wish. Miller's Esquire, a parti-color whelped in 1938, was both a bench show and a field trial champion, and also was awarded the C.D. and C.D.X obedience titles, the only Cocker to have won titles in all three areas. Prince Tom III, an ASCOB Cocker owned and trained by Tom Clute, earned his Utility Dog title in obedience and went on to win the title of National Field Trial Champion Cocker Spaniel of 1956.

In 1957 the American Spaniel Club offered a prize of $500 for the first Cocker Spaniel winning a dual title and $1,000 for the first Cocker winning a triple title. The $500 award was won by Ch. Minnopa's Mardi Gras U.D.T., owned by Adelaide L. Arntsen, and obedience trained by Russell Klipple.

It is interesting to note that the Best in Show winner at the American Spaniel Club National Specialty in January 1978 was the black bitch Am. and Can. Ch. Tabaka's Tidbit O'Wynden, who has also earned her C.D. and C.D.X. titles. She is owned by Ruth N. Tabaka and Laura Watt O'Connor.

In the late 1970s the American Kennel Club introduced an Obedience Trial Championship, eligibility for which was limited to dogs that already had their Utility Dog title. The first Cocker to win the OT title (he was already a bench champion) was OT Ch. and Ch. Mar-Lee's Folly O'Blarney, U.D., a red, whelped 1973, bred-owned-trained and shown by Mary Lee Whiting of Minneapolis.

Sterling Silver Beau, owned by Dennis and Louise Blake.

15

The Cocker Spaniel as a Hunting Dog

THE INTEREST in field work for the Cocker Spaniel constitutes an up and down graph over the years.

In 1904, there were only two field trials held in the whole country. In 1913, there were six. In 1918, 18. During this period the use of Spaniels in England was becoming more popular and the interest passed over to America.

It was largely due to a sportswoman, Mrs. Ella B. Moffit, that the Hunting Cocker Spaniel Club of America (soon to change its name to the present Cocker Spaniel Field Trial Club of America) was created and its first field trial held at Verbank, N.Y. in 1924. The judges were William Hutchinson and A. Clinton Wilmerding and there were three stakes: puppy, novice and all-age.

Mrs. Moffit later wrote of the trial, "We had so few dogs to run that each stake was practically a repeat . . . The puppy stake was won by Rowcliffe Diana, which I had acquired from a French Canadian only two weeks previous to the trials. Only seven months old, she was so small she provoked merriment from the gallery . . . but the way she retrieved a full grown cock pheasant bigger than herself turned the ridicule to respect and thus began a new era for the Cocker Spaniel in America."

Mrs. Evelyn Monte Van Horn, one of America's most respected field-trial judges and to whom we are indebted for much of the information here, tells of how from the very beginning, trials held by the Cocker Club included stakes for Springers. Likewise the Springer

271

Field Trial Champion Dungarvan Gunner's Delight retrieving a pheasant at the 1957 National Cocker Spaniel Field Championship. Note that owner Peter Garvan's gun is properly "broken", an essential caution for field trialers.

clubs held Cocker stakes. Springer field trial enthusiasts were strong supporters of the events held by the Cocker Club and have remained so throughout the history of spaniel trials.

Active participants in Cocker trials included the late all-rounder judge, E. Roland Harriman, whose Cinar Kennels at Arden, N.Y. gave name to the famous Cinar Trophy, Mr. and Mrs. Henry Berol, whose Berol Lodge Kennels at Chappaqua, N.Y. was breeding grounds for many field trial champions, Albert F. Winslow, Lillian and John Jacobsen, Dr. J. Richard Jones, John Mangine and Ted Young, Sr. For ten consecutive years there was a National Cocker Championship, the first held at Herrin, Ill., the last at Amwell, N.J. However, this interest did not continue.

Today's Cocker in the Field

Hastened by the war years, field trials fell into a decline from 1934 to 1945 but in the next few years there was a strong rebirth of interest in field bred and field trained Cockers. Ralph Craig, then president of the American Spaniel Club, put forth a great effort to revive the activity. Between 1958 and 1968 the ASC offered some marvelous prizes to the first Cocker to acquire the three titles of bench champion, obedience UDT degree and field trial champion. ($1,000 was offered to the winner of all three, and $500 to the winner of two championships.) In some of the Eastern field trials during the 1950s and early '60s, entries in the Cocker All Age outnumbered those in the Springer stake.

First to gain a field championship in the new era was Dungarvan Ready Teddy. Dungarvan Kennels was owned at the time by Mrs. Francis P. Garvan, and later by Mr. and Mrs. Peter Garvan. Peter died of a heart attack but his wife still raises field-bred Cockers along with her renowned field trial Springers. In the days of Cocker trials, Mrs. Garvan ran a number of winning dogs, finished the title of her Dungarvan Gunner's Delight, retired the LASHA trophy and won best amateur and best lady handler awards at the National Cocker Championship.

A diehard Cocker man who uses only Cockers for hunting is Hartwell S. (Bucky) Moore. Bucky ran field trial Cockers which he owned, trained and handled himself. He had: Fld. Ch. Fellers Freckles, winner of the Cinar Trophy 1951 and '52, Sports Afield All American Shooting Dog 1956, National Shooting Dog Championship 1958; and National Fld. Ch. Berol's Buckaroo, winner of the Cinar Trophy 1960 and the National Shooting Dog Championship 1959, '60 and '61.

The field Cocker personified by the 1962 National Field Champion Ru-Chars High Jinks. Bred and owned by the Greenings' Ru-Char Kennels, and trained by Luke Medlin.

High Jinks pictured with his owner-handler, Ruth Greening. He was by Fld. Ch. Ru-Char's Citation ex Fld. Ch. Ru-Char's Bess Again.

274

Charles and Ruth Greening, raising and running top-winning field trial Springers today at their Ru-Char Kennels in New Jersey campaigned many homebred Cockers of note. Among them: Fld. Ch. Ru-Char's Bess Again, Fld. Ch. Ru-Char's Citation and Fld. Ch. and National Fld. Ch. Ru-Char's High Jinks, all handled by Ruth.

Today, it is the feeling of many that the Cocker has not lost his hunting instinct but that the main problem is the excessive coat. For some, this beauty is more important than hunting in the field.

It would seem that this problem could be solved if our present standard was adhered to as it is written. The Cocker could retain his beauty and still be the sporting dog that he was intended to be originally. The standard reads: "The ears, chest, abdomen and legs are well feathered, but not so *excessively* as to hide the Cocker Spaniel's true lines and movement or affect his appearance and function as a *sporting dog*. . . . *Excessive* or curly or cottony textured coat is to be penalized."

Just Plain Autumn, owned by Steve and Vickie Dell, and Ch. Don's Dartanun, owned by Don Ploke.

275

Ch. Don's Dartanun.

His first field lesson. Windridge Chocolate Cyclone at the Orange County Cocker Club training classes in April 1975.

276

Recently there has been some activity in field trial work in two areas, California and New Jersey. We are indebted to Mr. Frank S. Wood, chairman of the Field Trial Committee of the American Spaniel Club, for this updated report:

Current activity in field work for the Cocker Spaniel has been somewhat limited. The strongest interest has been shown by the Cocker Spaniel Club of Orange County in California. It is interesting to note that about half of their training class is composed of English Cockers and one or two Clumber Spaniels.

The Field Trial Director of this club has spent many hours working with a local Springer Spaniel Club, learning and relating his learning to the Cocker Club members. The Springer Club has been most helpful, and allows the Cockers to run on their fun field days.

There are Cocker fanciers all over the country seeking guidance in field training their dogs. To these people, I strongly suggest contacting a local Springer Club for help and guidance.

It was my pleasure as Field Trial Chairman for 1976 to present to the Board at the October meeting in St. Louis, Working Dog and Working Dog Excellent rules, which were accepted and approved. WD and WDX rules should not be confused with the AKC Field Trial Rules. The WD and WDX Certificates are offered by the parent club. The American Spaniel Club had these rules several years ago.

The purpose of the WD and WDX Certificates is to keep the Cocker in the field and working—not necessarily in field trials, but it is a great start.

The rules have been circulated to all American Spaniel Club members and newly elected members. Extra copies are available for those who are interested. They are the same rules adopted and used by the parent clubs of the Springer and English Cocker.

For those who wish, you may enter your Cocker Spaniel in the WD and WDX trials for other flushing spaniel breeds. Have your score card signed by the judge and marked "passed," and have the Secretary forward it to the Secretary of the American Spaniel Club. The Rules state scores are to be sent to the Secretary of the Field Trial Committee Chairman. I do not know which procedure is correct, but in either case I am sure a WD or WDX Certificate will be forwarded to you.

Better yet, get your own club going with its own WD and WDX trials. The Cocker Spaniel Club of Orange County is very fortunate to have such a member as Ralph Miser who has taken so much of his time to teach the field class. Ralph and his wife, Jean, raise German

A 7 months old Ru-Char Cocker learning to retrieve.

Field enthusiasts Dennis Blake, Frank Wood and Ralph Miser.

Shorthair Pointers. They have had Cockers in the past and would like to see a Cocker Field Trial some day. Ralph is a professional dog trainer for all Sporting breeds in the field.

In follow-up to Mr. Wood's report, two Cockers have recently been awarded WDX certificates in the East.

On May 29, 1977, the Maryland Sporting Dog Association allowed Cocker Spaniels to be tested for the WD certificate, the first time any group agreed to test Cockers.

The entry of Cockers consisted of 4 English Cockers and an American Cocker. The following titles were awarded: WDX to the American Cocker, WDX to two of the English Cockers and a WD to one other English Cocker.

The American Cocker to win this honor was Sweet Sandy V, a year old bitch, owned, trained and handled by Alex and Pat Kovacs, Black Brook Farm, Hampton N.J. Sandy scored on her first try and thus became the first American Cocker to win a field award in many years.

A half year later, on October 14, 1977, a second Cocker was issued a WDX certificate. This award was won by Be Gay's Little Caesar, owned and trained by 14 year old Paula Pietrucha, with the assistance of Mr. and Mrs. Kovacs.

If this renewal of interest continues we can be sure that the Cocker Spaniel can and will return to eminence in the field.

Ch. My Own Brucie, black, whelped 1935, was one of the most popular of all American show dogs and did much to put the Cocker in the public eye. When he died in 1943, the "New York Evening Sun" published his obituary on the front page. Brucie's great winning included Best in Show at Morris-and-Essex in 1939 (over an entry of 4,456 dogs that long stood as an American record) and back-to-back wins of Best in Show at Westminster in 1940 and 1941. He is pictured being shown by his breeder-owner Herman E. Mellenthin to a win under breeder-judge Mrs. Arthur Vogel (later Mrs. Matthew Imrie).

16

Cocker Spaniel Clubs

THE American Spaniel Club has the distinction of being the first Specialty Club devoted entirely to one breed in this country and perhaps the Old World. The Club came into existence in 1881. There were 15 Charter members. Mr. A. H. Moore of Philadelphia was President.

When the American Spaniel Club joined the American Kennel Club, which it preceded by several years, it was accepted and thereafter recognized as the parent club of all Sporting Spaniels, a role and responsibility it assumed. However, it later became necessary to relinquish jurisdiction over some of the Sporting Spaniels as the popularity of the Cocker Spaniel became greater and others of the Spaniel family became more active on their own.

The first to leave the parent club was the English Springer Spaniel and others followed. The last to leave was the English Cocker Spaniel. The American Kennel Club had lumped the Cocker and the English Cocker together in its classification until 1945 and it is possible that the two were interbred to some extent during that time. The decision to separate the two breeds was an excellent one and today both clubs are proceeding on their own and doing well.

The American Spaniel Club retained the privilege of holding an All Spaniel Specialty Show every year. The only Sporting Spaniel not permitted entry in this show is the Brittany which, while called a Spaniel, is really a Setter.

It was in 1920 that the American Spaniel Club began holding an annual specialty show, early each January, at the Roosevelt Hotel in

A historic dog in a historic picture. Ch. Clarkdale Capital Stock, sire of 71 champions, winner of 17 all-breed Bests in Show and 25 Specialties, pictured in his win of Best in Show at the American Spaniel Club national Specialty of 1960. The judge is Mrs. M. Hartley Dodge (of Giralda and Morris & Essex fame). The handler is Howard Reno, awarding the trophy is Dr. John Eash, and the man absorbed at right is famous show superintendent George F. Foley. Capital Stock was bred and owned by Mr. and Mrs. Leslie Clark.

Robert W. Biggs, whose contributions to Cocker Spaniel progress date over many years is pictured here in 1968, when as president of the American Spaniel Club he presented a gift of appreciation to Clyde C. Seymour, judge of the regular classes at the club's national Specialty show.

New York City. The Futurity Stake was introduced to the fancy in 1923 and has continued ever since.

On January 10th, 1944, the American Spaniel Club radically amended its Constitution and By-Laws to make the Club's government more representative. The purpose of these changes was to encourage the various sections of the country to increase their membership in the Club. Four Zones were established and the management of the Club was placed under the jurisdiction of an Executive Committee.

The Zone system was a success and members began to join from all over the country. My husband, Lee, served as Zone Representative for Zone 3 during the first four years of the zoning system, 1944 to 1948. He took a very active part during those early days and it was his pleasure to know and work with Judge Townsend Scudder, a great judge and a real asset to the Club.

Since then, through elections, there have been many changes in the Club personnel, all endeavoring to carry on the work incidental to running a successful club. In 1960, I was elected Representative for Zone 3 and held that office for 12 years. During the past decade the popularity of the Cocker Spaniel has increased tremendously with the result

Master Sgt. Bode, Cocker Spaniel, with 16 parachute jumps to his credit! The dog, bred at the author's Silver Maple Kennels, was owned by Sgt. First Class Hubert Huth of the Eighteenth Airborne Corps Artillery. Sgt. Huth was a veteran of 12 years in the Army and made 72 parachute jumps. The dog was the company mascot. Sgt. Huth taught his Cocker to make jumps without injury. The dog learned to fall relaxed after six months training, and when he hit the ground, he would sit on his parachute so that the wind would not blow him away. He also did some winning at the dog shows. He was 13 years old when this picture was taken and was getting quite gray.

that the Cocker is at this writing, in 1982, again in the position of No. 1 Sporting Dog in the nation, and No. 2 of all-breeds.

The rapid growth of the membership is indicated by the following: in 1881 there were 15 Charter members; in 1925 there were 65 members, in 1943 there were 200 members; in 1945, just two years after the Zones were established, there were 400 members; in 1959 there were over 600 and at the present time, there are over 1100 voting members.

In December 1957 the American Kennel Club approved an important change in the height Standard. This was a change from the former weight requirement to the height specification which is in effect today and has proven much more satisfactory. This was given "teeth" via a disqualification clause in the Standard. The size of the Cocker Spaniel almost immediately began to show more uniformity.

There was a noticeable effort at this time to bring the height of the Cocker down quickly in order to meet the Standard and avoid disqualification. This gave the Cocker a long, low look, which disappeared in just a few years, and the Cocker began to come up on leg noticeably. This brought about the question of an obsolete Standard that did not meet the present Cocker.

In 1972, I was appointed Chairman of a new Standard Committee, and asked for the appointment of Ted Young on the East Coast and Mary Doty on the West Coast to serve with me. Club president Robert Walker served as ex-officio member. The committee worked hard to bring the obsolete standard up to date. The changes proposed were approved by the American Kennel Club, and the new standard became effective February 1, 1973.

In 1981, further changes — specifically on Color and Markings, including putting the black and tan variety with the Blacks,—were made in the standard to become effective January 1, 1982. The standard as printed elsewhere in this book contains these changes.

The Board of Directors, after a two year study and survey, added an additional Zone to the four Zones set up in 1946. Zone 5, the New Zone, comprises the states of Missouri, Arkansas, Oklahoma, Texas and Kansas.

Although the Constitution and Charter Committee worked many hours preparing a Charter of Incorporation and a set of By-Laws for the Club, the two-thirds majority of the voting members proved difficult to get. It was not until October 7, 1974, that the Non-Profit Articles of Incorporation were accepted. The new By-Laws to conform were approved by the AKC on October 30, 1975.

Ch. Biggs Believe It Or Not, whose call name was "Ripley" in recognition of the cartoonist who originated the famous "Believe It Or Not" newspaper feature, is pictured with Mr. Robert Ripley himself. Whelped in 1950, the dog was so named because it was the first time that the Biggs had come up with a black/tan Cocker. He was a good one and won the National Specialty. At right is the Biggs' son, Robert.

A National Cocker Spaniel Summer Show, to be held each year in different locations, was decided upon in 1975. The location for the first summer show was Oklahoma City on July 16th and 17th, 1977. Great interest was shown and there was a fine entry and a most successful show. In 1978, this show is planned for the West Coast.

April 1, 1976, the American Spaniel Club established their first Annual Health Registry. The purpose is to give members an opportunity to voluntarily list as normal one or more of four life threatening defects that could affect Cocker Spaniels: Cataracts; Progressive Retinal Atrophy; Factor 10 and Hip Dysplasia. If a dog is not listed for all defects, it does not preclude that animal is defective for these absent defects. It is suggested that the eye examinations be made once a year, as the tests only indicate freedom from the defects on the date tested and provide no information on the future status of the dog's eyes.

This is a worthy endeavor on the part of the American Spaniel Club to assist in reducing the number of these defects and the breeders are cooperating to a great degree.

In 1981, the American Spaniel Club celebrated its one hundredth year with issuance of *"A Century of Spaniels"*, a glorious two-volume assemblage of historic pictures and facts, masterfully compiled by a staff headed by Frances Greer as editor-in-chief.

The Cocker Spaniel fancy is very fortunate in having available two magazines whose publishers are dedicated to the breed. *The American Cocker Review* has been in operation for some twenty years and the Editor and Publisher, Mari and Norman Doty are, themselves, breeders of Cocker Spaniels. They are keeping its readers well informed on Cocker activities. *The Cocker Spaniel Leader,* a newer magazine edited and published by Gene and Shirley Estel, is also doing a good job for the fancy. The Estels, too, are breeders of Cocker Spaniels with a sincere interest in the breed.

The tremendous increase in the number of Cockers registered each month, as shown in the *American Kennel Gazette,* is almost alarming. While we are happy to know that our lovely Cocker is so popular, there is still the danger of over-population. This is often caused by the greed of those interested more in monetary gains rather than improvement of the breed.

This is just a word of caution to breeders.

BIBLIOGRAPHY

ALL OWNERS of pure-bred dogs will benefit themselves and their dogs by enriching the knowledge of breeds and of canine care, training, breeding, psychology and other important aspec of dog management. The following list of books covers further reading recommended by judge veterinarians, breeders, trainers and other authorities. Books may be obtained at the finer boc stores and pet shops, or through Howell Book House Inc., publishers, New York.

Breed Books

AFGHAN HOUND, Complete	Miller & Gilbert
AIREDALE, New Complete	Edwards
AKITA, Complete	Linderman & Funk
ALASKAN MALAMUTE, Complete	Riddle & Seeley
BASSET HOUND, Complete	Braun
BEAGLE, New Complete	Noted Authorities
BLOODHOUND, Complete	Brey & Reed
BORZOI, Complete	Groshans
BOXER, Complete	Denlinger
BRITTANY SPANIEL, Complete	Riddle
BULLDOG, New Complete	Hanes
BULL TERRIER, New Complete	Eberhard
CAIRN TERRIER, Complete	Marvin
CHESAPEAKE BAY RETRIEVER, Complete	Cherry
CHIHUAHUA, Complete	Noted Authorities
COCKER SPANIEL, New	Kraeuchi
COLLIE, New	Official Publication of the
	Collie Club of America
DACHSHUND, The New	Meistrell
DALMATIAN, The	Treen
DOBERMAN PINSCHER, New	Walker
ENGLISH SETTER, New Complete	Tuck, Howell & Graef
ENGLISH SPRINGER SPANIEL, New	Goodall & Gasow
FOX TERRIER, New Complete	Silvernail
GERMAN SHEPHERD DOG, New Complete	Bennett
GERMAN SHORTHAIRED POINTER, New	Maxwell
GOLDEN RETRIEVER, Complete	Fischer
GREAT DANE, New Complete	Noted Authorities
GREAT DANE, The—Dogdom's Apollo	Draper
GREAT PYRENEES, Complete	Strang & Giffin
IRISH SETTER, New	Thompson
IRISH WOLFHOUND, Complete	Starbuck
KEESHOND, Complete	Peterson
LABRADOR RETRIEVER, Complete	Warwick
LHASA APSO, Complete	Herbel
MINIATURE SCHNAUZER, Complete	Eskrigge
NEWFOUNDLAND, New Complete	Chern
NORWEGIAN ELKHOUND, New Complete	Wallo
OLD ENGLISH SHEEPDOG, Complete	Mandeville
PEKINGESE, Quigley Book of	Quigley
PEMBROKE WELSH CORGI, Complete	
	Sargent & Harper
POODLE, New Complete	Hopkins & Irick
POODLE CLIPPING AND GROOMING BOOK,	
Complete	Kalstone
PULI, Complete	Owen
SAMOYED, Complete	Ward
SCHIPPERKE, Official Book of	Root, Martin, Kent
SCOTTISH TERRIER, New Complete	Marvin
SHETLAND SHEEPDOG, The New	Riddle
SHIH TZU, Joy of Owning	Seranne
SHIH TZU, The (English)	Dadds
SIBERIAN HUSKY, Complete	Demidoff
TERRIERS, The Book of All	Marvin
WEST HIGHLAND WHITE TERRIER,	
Complete	Marvin
WHIPPET, Complete	Pegram
YORKSHIRE TERRIER, Complete	Gordon & Bennett

Breeding

ART OF BREEDING BETTER DOGS, New	Onst…
BREEDING YOUR OWN SHOW DOG	Serann…
HOW TO BREED DOGS	Whitn…
HOW PUPPIES ARE BORN	Pri…
INHERITANCE OF COAT COLOR IN DOGS	Litt…

Care and Training

DOG OBEDIENCE, Complete Book of	Saunde…
NOVICE, OPEN AND UTILITY COURSES	Saunde…
DOG CARE AND TRAINING FOR BOYS	
AND GIRLS	Saunde…
DOG NUTRITION, Collins Guide to	Colli…
DOG TRAINING FOR KIDS	Benjam…
DOG TRAINING, Koehler Method of	Koeh…
DOG TRAINING, Step by Step Manual	Volhard & Fish…
GO FIND! Training Your Dog to Track	Da…
GUARD DOG TRAINING, Koehler Method of	Koeh…
OPEN OBEDIENCE FOR RING, HOME	
AND FIELD, Koehler Method of	Koeh…
STONE GUIDE TO DOG GROOMING FOR	
ALL BREEDS	Sto…
SUCCESSFUL DOG TRAINING, The	
Pearsall Guide to	Pears…
TOY DOGS, Kalstone Guide to Grooming All	Kalsto…
TRAINING THE RETRIEVER	Kers…
TRAINING YOUR DOG TO WIN OBEDIENCE	
TITLES	Mors…
TRAIN YOUR OWN GUN DOG, How to	Good…
UTILITY DOG TRAINING, Koehler Method of	Koeh…
VETERINARY HANDBOOK, Dog Owner's Home	
	Carlson & Gi…

General

CANINE TERMINOLOGY	Sp…
COMPLETE DOG BOOK, The	Official Publication…
	American Kennel Cl…
DOG IN ACTION, The	Ly…
DOG BEHAVIOR, New Knowledge of	Pfaffenber…
DOG JUDGE'S HANDBOOK	Tiet…
DOG JUDGING, Nicholas Guide to	Nicho…
DOG PEOPLE ARE CRAZY	Rid…
DOG PSYCHOLOGY	Whitr…
DOGSTEPS, Illustrated Gait at a Glance	Ell…
DOG TRICKS	Haggerty & Benjan…
ENCYCLOPEDIA OF DOGS, International	
	Dangerfield, Howell & Rid…
FROM RICHES TO BITCHES	Shatt…
IN STITCHES OVER BITCHES	Shatt…
JUNIOR SHOWMANSHIP HANDBOOK	Brown & Mas…
MY TIMES WITH DOGS	Fletc…
OUR PUPPY'S BABY BOOK (blue or pink)	
SUCCESSFUL DOG SHOWING, Forsyth Guide to	Fors…
TRIM, GROOM AND SHOW YOUR DOG, How to	
	Saund…
WHY DOES YOUR DOG DO THAT?	Bergm…
WILD DOGS in Life and Legend	Rid…
WORLD OF SLED DOGS, From Siberia to Sport Racin…	
	Coppin…